Permanent Results
without
Permanent Dieting
WORKBOOK

Weight Loss Method

by
Health and Nutrition Counselor
Gary Heavin

Founder & C.E.O., Curves International Inc.
The World's Largest Fitness Center Franchise

Book Design by: Janet Bergin, Mean Mommy Publishing
Recipe Development and Editing by: Cathy Bergin, Mean Mommy Publishing

CONTENTS

He who enjoys good health is rich,
though he knows it not.

—Italian Proverb

Dear Curves Member,

We hope this workbook helps you to better understand the process of healthy and permanent weight loss. Our approach is unique in that we define dieting as a temporary condition. We protect lean tissue through strength training and by consuming adequate amounts of protein while dieting. We effectively deal with the metabolic changes that occur as a result of weight loss efforts. This will enable you to then deal with the small amount of weight gain that caused your weight problem.

Knowledge is power. A thorough understanding of all of the factors regarding weight loss will give you the power over your weight and health. Our intent is to inform as well as motivate you during the next six weeks. Commit yourself to this program. Realize that important goals require effort and even discomfort. You can do it. You're worth the effort.

Gary Heavin,
Founder & C.E.O.
Curves International, Inc.

~

RESOURCES

~

MEASUREMENT CHART

Keeping track of your progress is important.

WEEK 1 - BEGINNING MEASUREMENTS

Bust _____
Waist_____
Abdomen _____
Hip _____
Thigh_____
Calf _____
Arm _____
Weight _____
Body fat % _____
Fat lbs. _____
Date _____

WEEK 4 - MEASUREMENTS

Bust _____
Waist_____
Abdomen _____
Hip _____
Thigh_____
Calf _____
Arm _____
Weight _____
Body fat % _____
Fat lbs. _____
Date _____

FINAL MEASUREMENTS

Bust _____
Waist_____
Abdomen _____
Hip _____
Thigh_____
Calf _____
Arm _____
Weight _____
Body fat % _____
Fat lbs. _____
Date _____

GOAL MEASUREMENTS

Bust _____
Waist_____
Abdomen _____
Hip _____
Thigh_____
Calf _____
Arm _____
Weight _____
Body fat % _____
Fat lbs. _____
Date _____

WEIGHT LOSS CHART

Write your beginning weight in the top box in the left column and enter one pound decreases down the column. Place an X in the corresponding weekly weight amounts. Place your goal weight in the goal box. This graph will help you visualize your success.

Start   **Goal**

Weight	Week 2	Week 3	Week 4	Week 5	Week 6	Week 7	
186							
185	X						
184							
183							
182		X					
181							
180			X				

Start   **Goal**

Weight	Week 2	Week 3	Week 4	Week 5	Week 6	Week 7	

EXERCISE CHART

Keep a record of weekly exercise. Each day place an X in the box for each ten minutes of exercise performed. Write the type of exercise and how much energy you felt afterward, on a scale of 1 to 5, with 5 being the highest.

Week #	Day or Date	Minutes per day Each box = 10 minutes								Type of Exercise	Post Exercise Energy Level 1 to 5 (most)

TEST I

SYMPTOMS OF
CARBOHYDRATE INTOLERANCE

(Check any symptoms you experience on a regular basis)

____Nervousness

____Irritability

____Fatigue and exhaustion

____Faintness, dizziness, cold sweats, shakiness, weak spells

____Depression

____Drowsiness, especially after meals or in mid-afternoon

____Headaches

____Digestive disturbances with no apparent cause

____Forgetfulness

____Insomnia

____Needless worry

____Mental confusion

____Rapid pulse, especially after eating certain foods

____Muscle pains

____Antisocial behavior

____Overly emotional crying spells

____Lack of sex drive

____Leg cramps and blurred vision

____Shortness of breath, sighing and excess yawning

____Cravings for starch and sugar-rich foods

____**Total**

TEST II

CARBOHYDRATE INTOLERANCE

(Check all statements that apply to you)

____You are more than 25 pounds overweight

____You have had a tendency to be overweight all of your life

____You have been overweight since you were a child

____You have a poor appetite and often skip meals

____You have food cravings that temporarily go away when starchy or sugary foods are eaten

____There are foods that you feel you absolutely could not do without

____Your waist is bigger than your hips

____You checked most or all of the symptoms on Test 1

____**Total**

~

TEST III

CALORIE SENSITIVITY

(Check all statements that apply to you)

____You had a normal body weight when younger but slowly gained weight after age 30

____You are presently overweight, but by less than 25 pounds

____You have a normal appetite and get hungry at meal times

____You have few, if any, food cravings

____You have maintained the same basic eating habits all of your life

____You eat three meals per day

____You have gained a certain amount of extra body weight but seem to have tapered off (not continued to steadily gain more and more weight)

____You checked few or none of the symptoms on Test 1

____**Total**

PHASE I

Phase I is the strictest part of the plan. You will choose the most advantageous method of dieting for you, based on the tests on pages 9 and 10. If the tests show that you are carbohydrate intolerant, you may enjoy the advantage of a higher protein and lower carbohydrate plan. The advantage of this plan is that you can eat more food and still lose weight. However, you must limit your carbohydrates to 20 grams per day (after subtracting free foods).

If the tests show that you are calorie sensitive, you must eat fewer calories, as well as limiting carbohydrates. The calorie sensitive plan calls for 1200 calories and 60 grams of carbohydrates per day (after subtracting free foods).

If you are one of the 25% who seem to be both carbohydrate and calorie sensitive, you may start with the higher protein plan. If you haven't lost any weight within a few days, go to the calorie restricted plan, or if your weight loss stops following several weeks of success with the higher protein plan, move to the calorie restricted plan.

Stay on the stricter Phase I plan for one or two weeks depending on the amount of weight you need to lose. If you have less than twenty pounds to lose, one week is sufficient. If you have twenty or more pounds to lose, two weeks is appropriate.

It is very motivating to lose weight quickly. However, for periods longer than two weeks, you need wider variety and larger amounts of food than Phase I provides. Phase I will allow you to acquire the skill and confidence to lose weight when you need to. This tool is an important part of Phase III.

Enjoy your free foods and the variety they provide. One Curves shake per day (made with skim milk) will give you a moment of pleasure by providing a treat.

TEST RESULTS

If you agreed with more statements on Test II, (the carbohydrate-intolerance quiz), you should be successful on a higher-protein diet. If you agreed with more statements on Test III, (the calorie-sensitive quiz), you should restrict your calorie intake. If you agreed with a similar number on both, you can probably start with a higher protein diet and enjoy its advantages, but you will need to restrict calories later to continue losing weight.

THE PHYSIOLOGY OF FITNESS

1. **Curves Workout Philosophy**
   Optimal health and weight control are dependent on each of the five areas of a total workout.
   - warm up
   - twenty minutes of sustained target heart rate (cardio)
   - three sets of strength training on all major muscle groups
   - cool down
   - stretching (elasticity)

2. **Strength Training**
   Strength training requires you to move a greater resistance than you are accustomed to. This progressive increase in resistance stimulates the muscle to increase in size and strength, which raises metabolism.
   a. Muscle vs. Fat
      - A pound of muscle burns about 50 calories per day at rest
      - A pound of fat burns almost no calories because it is always at rest
      - A larger muscle mass results in a higher metabolism
      - Muscles provide greater stability to help prevent you from falling or injuring yourself if you do fall
      - Strong muscles provide joint support
   b. Hydraulic resistance advantages
      - Safe, like aquatic exercise
      - Resistance is determined by speed: faster = more resistance
      - Pushing and pulling instead of lifting and lowering
      - Fewer injuries compared with weights
      - Opposing muscles are worked symmetrically
      - Eliminates almost all soreness
      - Muscle will firm its full length

3. **Aerobics (Cardio)**
   If you perform an activity that raises your heart rate to a training or "target" level and sustain that rate for more than ten minutes, you are working aerobically.
   a. Target heart rate
      - 220 - age = maximum heart rate
        maximum heart rate x 50% to 80% = target heart rate
      - Check heart rate by counting your carotid (neck) or radial (wrist), or heart (chest) pulse
      - Curves Workout system utilizes a ten second heart rate count. Check the wall chart for target rates according to age

    b. Aerobic advantages
- Aerobic means "with oxygen"
- Essential for burning stored fat
- Improves entire cardio-respiratory system: heart, lungs and vascular system

    c. Anaerobic disadvantages
- Anaerobic means "without oxygen"
- Burns only glucose in the blood stream and glycogen in the muscles—not stored fat

    d. Perceived exertion
- If you are breathing deeply but are able to maintain a conversation during exercise, you are working at an appropriate level of intensity
- If you are gasping for air, you are working too hard
- Use this method if you are taking blood pressure medication

    e. Key to aerobic exercise is FIT
- **F**requency: at least 3 times per week
- **I**ntensity: at your target heart rate
- **T**ime: at target heart rate for a minimum of 20 minutes

    f. Importance of warm up
- Increases blood flow to muscles
- Allows oxygen quicker access to muscles
- Speeds up breakdown of glucose and fatty acids
- Makes muscles more elastic and less susceptible to injury
- Reduces heart irregularities associated with sudden exertion
- More easily burns fat

    g. Importance of cool down
- Allows your heart rate to gradually slow down and adjust back to normal
- If you suddenly stop after a workout, you could become dizzy or lightheaded, or possibly even lose consciousness
- Majority of severe cardiac irregularities that can be dangerous occur following the exercise, not during it

4. **Stretching**

    a. Benefits
- Decreased risk of injury
- Enhanced joint integrity
- Increased blood supply and nutrients to joint structures
- Better balance, coordination and situational awareness
- Decreased risk of low back pain

    b. Technique
- <u>Gently</u> stretch muscles, no jerky or bouncing motions
- Hold each stretch for 15 seconds

CHAPTER 2

UNDERSTANDING WEIGHT GAIN

1. **You don't have to diet forever**
   a. Gradual weight gain
      - average gain of 3 pounds per year
      - $1/2$ pound = 1750 calories
      - $1/2$ pound per month weight gain is easily avoided
   b. Pregnancy weight gain
      - weight gain is hormonal
      - breast feeding is a weight loss advantage
   c. Our amazing body
      - protects us from gaining a huge amount (most of us should be hundreds of pounds overweight)
      - There are chemical factors and influences that affect body weight beyond exercise and calorie intake
2. **Plateau**
   a. Starvation
      - Our bodies have a safety mechanism that helps to protect us from starvation. When you are on a diet that allows you to burn stored energy, your body senses starvation. Dieting is simulated starvation from your body's perspective.
   b. Metabolism
      - Metabolism increases as people eat more and decreases as people eat less
      - Metabolism attempts to adapt to caloric intake.
      - The maintenance diet of most conventional weight loss programs condemns you to a perpetually lower metabolism and perpetual dieting

CHAPTER 3

OUR PAST AFFECTS OUR PRESENT

1. **Designed for survival**
   a. Weight cycling
      - People, like most other mammals, ate well during warmer months and gained extra body weight for nutrition and insulation to survive the winter
      - Carbohydrates were more abundant during summer months
      - Carbohydrates stimulate insulin, which is the hormone that enables us to store energy in the fat cell

- During the winter, people were able to exist on protein and fat and burn stored energy safely
- There is no evidence that weight cycling in humans has adverse effects on body composition, energy expenditure, risk factors for cardiovascular disease, or the effectiveness of future efforts at weight loss
- We were designed to be in a fat-storing mode for periods of time and a fat-burning mode for others

  b. Prehistoric humans
- Hunter gatherers usually had long, dense bones and strong teeth
- Agriculturists usually had worn and decayed teeth and frail and underdeveloped bones

2. **Three major changes in our diet since 1900**

  a Sugar
- Refined sugar has had all the nutrients removed
- Sugar is pure energy whose excess is available for storage
- Consuming sugar stimulates the production of insulin, which starts the fat-storing process

  b. Refined wheat and rice
- Refining grains eliminates the course roughage, which contains the fiber and many nutrients
- Chromium, an essential trace mineral, is over 90% destroyed in the refining process

  c. Vegetable oil
- Vegetable oil is polyunsaturated, and is usually considered by experts to be "safe"
- However, vegetable oil is molecularly unstable and is associated with free-radical damage

4. **Trading proteins for carbohydrates**
- Since the 1970s we have been avoiding fats and adding more carbohydrates to our diets
- Fat consumption dropped 17% while obesity increased by 25%

CHAPTER 4

NUTRITIONAL REVIEW

1. **We are what we eat**

  a. Protein
- One gram of protein contains 4 calories
- Proteins are strings of amino acids that the body utilizes to sustain tissue, to build muscle and other critical components, and to provide energy
- The human body is unable to make essential amino acids

- In the absence of essential amino acids, health is impaired.
- Complete proteins are found in meats, cheeses, eggs, seafood and poultry
- Incomplete proteins are found in vegetables, grains and nuts These proteins must be carefully combined to provide all the essential amino acids if you are not eating animal protein
- The minimum daily need for protein is from .5 to 1 gram per pound of body weight

b. Fats
- 1 gram of fat contains 9 calories
- Animal fats are considered saturated. They are solid at room temperature. They have a more stable molecular structure.
- Vegetable fats are considered unsaturated and are liquid at room temperature. They have a less stable molecular structure.
- Monounsaturated fats, such as olive oil, are more stable than vegetable oils and are considered to be healthier due to a lesser potential for oxidation and free-radical damage to cells.
- Fatty acids maintain the myelin sheath protecting nerves and are necessary to metabolize vitamins and provide energy.
- Linoleic acid is an essential fatty acid that can be derived from many foods.
- Omega fatty acids can be derived from certain fish or fish oils.

c. Carbohydrates
- 1 gram of carbohydrate contains 4 calories
- Carbohydrates are essentially sugars
- Fructose is the sugar from fruit
- Sucrose comes from plants such as sugarcane or sugar beets
- Lactose is the sugar present in milk
- All carbohydrates are converted into glucose, which is the form in which your body can utilize them
- Carbohydrates stimulate the production of insulin
- Many people are addicted to carbohydrates and their consumption leads to overeating and obesity

d. Fiber
- Fiber is the cellulose portion of plants that is not digested
- Soluble fiber forms a gel-like substance which expands and moves slowly through the upper digestive system. This gives you a feeling of fullness.
- Fiber moves food faster through the intestinal tract so that fewer calories are absorbed
- The National Cancer Institute recommends 30 grams of fiber daily
- Soluble fiber is found in oat products, dry beans, lentils and barley
- Insoluble fiber does not dissolve in water
- Insoluble fiber comes from the outer hard shell of grains and is found in most fruits and vegetables. Bran, celery, green beans, green leafy vegetables, potato skins and whole grains are a good source.

CHAPTER 5

LIVING ON STORED ENERGY

1. **Most members need not diet**
   a. By eliminating sugar and starting an aerobic and strength training program, many of our members reach their goals without having to diet
2. **Higher protein opportunity**
   a. Higher protein, lower fat, lower carbohydrates
      - Ability to eat more and still lose weight
      - Protein burns slowly and gives us a steady source of energy and diminishes hunger
      - A high intake of protein provides amino acids to sustain metabolically active muscle tissue
      - Fat in food is satisfying and prolongs the feeling of fullness
3. **Understanding ketosis**
   a. The human brain utilizes glucose as its primary energy source. In the absence of carbohydrates and glucose your liver can alter fat so that it can be utilized as energy by your brain. These ketones are only partially burned and then excreted in urine, sweat or breath. If you are trying to burn off stored fat, this incomplete burning of fat results in a faster weight loss.
   b. Moderate ketosis is safe for people in good health as long as they drink adequate amounts of water to keep their kidneys flushed and get adequate nutrients to maintain their electrolytic balance
4. **Counting Calories**
   a. Approximately 25% of people do not lose weight on a high protein diet
      - Their bodies are able to utilize the energy available in protein and fats in the absence of carbohydrates
      - These people need to restrict calories to burn stored body fat
      - They need to eat higher protein, lower fat and lower carbohydrates to lose body fat effectively
   b. Another 25% of people are moderately carbohydrate intolerant
      - They may enjoy benefits of a higher-protein diet temporarily, but then they must begin to restrict calories in order to continue burning stored fat

CHAPTER 6

HORMONAL INFLUENCES

1. **Insulin**
   Insulin's job is to lower blood sugar levels by transporting the glucose into muscle cells to be used as energy. What cannot be used by the muscles is then taken to the fat cells for storage.
   a. lowers elevated blood sugar
   b. shifts metabolism into a storage mode
   c. converts glucose and protein into fat
   d. converts dietary fat to stored fat
   e. removes fats from blood and transports to fat cells
   f. increases the body's production of cholesterol
   g. makes the kidneys retain excess fluid
   h. stimulates the use of glucose for energy

2. **Glucagon**
   Glucagon makes energy available from the fat cells. As your blood sugar lowers, glucagon replenishes energy needs by facilitating the release of energy from stored fat.
   a. raises low blood sugar
   b. shifts metabolism into a burning mode
   c. converts dietary fats and stored fat to ketones for energy
   d. converts protein and fat into glucose
   e. releases fat from fat cells and makes it available for energy
   f. decreases the body's production of cholesterol
   g. makes the kidneys release excess fluid
   h. stimulates the use of fat for energy

3. **Lypogenic enzymes**
   "Lypo" means fat and "genic" means building. These enzymes facilitate the storage of fat. They allow the body to eke out the most energy from foods and resist the utilization of fat stores. The opposing lypolytic (fat break down) enzymes facilitate the utilization of fat from storage.
   a. Research from Cedars-Sinai hospital shows that the human body will begin to increase production of the lypogenic enzymes within 72 hours of dieting
   b. Seventy-two hours is the length of time you can diet and not restimulate the production of starvation hormones
   c. *Prevailing metabolism* is the body's broader response to dieting. Your body responds to behavior by attempting to maintain homeostasis or "like state."
   d. Homeostasis is a normal objective of many of the body's systems.

Fluid and pH balances are examples of carefully maintained processes of homeostasis that are necessary for survival.
   e. Resisting change is natural
4. **Starvation Hormones**
   a. Dieting is a simulated period of starvation
   b. The body becomes more efficient when sensing starvation. It resists change by slowing the loss of fat by lowering metabolism or producing "starvation hormones."
   c. Perpetual dieting adapts the body to a perpetually lower metabolism by lowering the *prevailing metabolism*
   d. Eating raises the *prevailing metabolism*

CHAPTER 7

PERMANENT RESULTS WITHOUT PERMANENT DIETING

1. **The Heavin Formula**
   a. A weight control method that is simple and effective in utilizing the hormonal factors of weight control
   b. You will know when it is time to diet and when it is not
   c. After losing the desired weight, you will be able to stabilize at the new weight and raise your metabolism
   d. You will deal with small weight gains before they can add up
2. **Phase I**
Many women lose between 5 and 10 pounds during the first two weeks. Some of this is water weight. It is important that you replenish these fluids by drinking adequate amounts of water. If you have less than 20 pounds to lose, spend just one week on Phase I. Otherwise, you will need two weeks on Phase I.
   a. **Calorie Restricted Version**
     • 40% or more of calories come from protein
     • No more than 60 grams of carbohydrates
     • 1,200 total calories per day
     • Unlimited free foods
     • 1 *Curves shake* (made with 8 ounces of skim milk) per day is considered a free food
     • 8 (8-ounce) glasses of water per day
     • A vitamin and mineral supplement such as *Curves Complete* each day
     • Coffee, tea, diet drinks and artificial sweeteners are allowed
   b. **Higher protein/Low Carbohydrate Version**
     • Unlimited protein, lower fat, 20 grams of carbohydrates

- Unlimited free foods
- 1 *Curves shake* (made with 8 ounces of skim milk) per day is considered a free food
- 8 (8-ounce) glasses of water per day
- A vitamin and mineral supplement such as *Curves Complete* each day
- Coffee, tea, diet drinks and artificial sweeteners are allowed

3. **Phase II**

   After one or two weeks on Phase I, you need to increase your food intake. You should expect to lose 1 to 2 pounds per week. Most people can safely lose body fat at that rate.

   a. Calorie Restricted Version
      - Increase your caloric intake to 1,600 calories per day
      - Keep carbohydrate grams to 60 grams per day
   b. Higher protein/Low Carbohydrate Version
      - Increase your carbohydrate grams to 60 grams per day
   c. You may stay on Phase II as long as you are losing weight.

4. **Plateau**

   If you spend more than a month or two dieting, your *prevailing metabolism* will decrease. When weight loss stops, this is your plateau. Lowering your caloric intake at this point is unhealthy. You should move on to Phase III.

5. **Phase III**

   The objective is to raise your metabolism to where it was before you started dieting but not gain the weight back. You need to begin eating to raise your *prevailing metabolism*. Most people stabilize at their new weight within a month or two.

   a. Begin eating normally again, even rewarding yourself for what you have accomplished
   b. Weigh yourself every day
   c. Don't panic—you will gain weight. You know how to lose weight when you need to. Allow a gain of 2 to 3 pounds or if you're a larger person perhaps up to 5 pounds.
   d. Discount normal monthly weight fluctuations
   e. As soon as the scale shows a gain of 3 pounds, go back to Phase I for 2 to 3 days
   f. At your low weight, begin eating again
   g. *The key is to diet just long enough to lose the small amount of weight you gained, but not long enough to restimulate the production of starvation hormones.*
   h. Notice that it takes a longer and longer amount of time to regain those pounds.

6. **Raising metabolism before dieting**

   If you have sabotaged your metabolism by yo-yo dieting or restricted eating, you may have to raise your metabolism before you can safely lose weight.

a. Spend one or two months on Phase III to raise your metabolism until you can eat a normal diet of 2,000-3,000 calories daily without gaining weight.
b. If you cannot lose weight eating less than 1,500 calories per day, you must begin with Phase III and raise your prevailing metabolism. After you have raised your prevailing metabolism to two or three thousand calories a day, you are ready to safely lose weight.
c. Many women who use the Curves Workout exercise system can lose up to 20 pounds of body fat in a year without dieting. By burning an additional 300 to 500 calories per day and performing resistance exercises to protect and increase muscles, they can expect significant and lasting change.

CHAPTER 8

NUTRITIONAL SUPPLEMENTATION

1. **Nutrients are the building blocks of a healthy body.**
   a. Vitamins are usually obtained from the foods we eat, but processing, cooking and canning destroy many nutrients.
   b. A deficiency of any nutrient can eventually manifest itself in disease.
   c. We should eat food in its natural state as much as possible, such as raw vegetables and fruit.
   d. Shopping the perimeter of the grocery store (vegetables, fruits, non-processed foods) is the best way to ensure you're getting healthy, natural foods.
2. **Soil deficiencies**
   a. The soils of America have declined in quality.
   b. We have been replacing only three minerals: nitrogen, phosphorus and potassium (NPK) for the last seventy years.
   c. Unhealthy plants require pesticides which have contaminated most of our food.
   d. Rampant chronic disease was predicted over seventy years ago based on the deficiency of minerals caused by farming methods.
3. **Recommended Dietary Allowances**
   a. Medical and nutritional journals are validating the need for supplementation, but health professionals have been very slow to respond.
   b. The recommended dietary allowance (RDA) is just over the minimal amount of a nutrient needed to prevent certain diseases.

c. Studies are consistently showing that adequate doses of vitamins are able to fend off disease.

4. **What does a woman's body need?**
    a. 10 to 12 amino acids
    b. 3 fatty acids
    c. 16 vitamins
    d. 70+ minerals
    e. phytonutrients
    f. heavy-hitting antioxidants

5. **Curves Nutritional Supplements**

    Out of necessity, Curves has formulated and developed five supplements for the unique needs of women.

    a. **Curves Complete**

        Provides the essential nutrients that are needed for a woman's optimal health.
        - All natural vitamins, no synthetics
        - The proper ratio of nutrients
        - An acidic base to enhance absorption
        - Plant-source trace minerals, recognizable by the body
        - Major minerals in a form for best absorption
        - Liquid form to allow for best absorption
        - Specific nutrients for a woman's needs

    b. **Curves Integrated**

        Provides nutrients to help maintain the integrity of joints.
        - Glucosamine
        - Chondroitin sulfates
        - Vitamin B-6
        - Trace minerals

    c. **Curves Essential**

        It includes the form of calcium and minerals which were proven in a double-blind study to actually restore bone density.

    d. **Curves Herbal FEM**

        Designed to support and maintain a woman's biochemistry during life's transitions.

    e. **Curves PMS Formula**

        This supplement helps to alleviate the symptoms of PMS by helping to balance the hormonal changes that occur during a woman's monthly cycle.

    f. **Curves shake**

        A delicious drink that is rich in nutrients including soy protein with isoflavones, a natural estrogen.
        - Contains 20 grams of protein and 20 grams of carbohydrates
        - Its herbal blend speeds the digestive process and helps to detoxify the body
        - Contains no artificial sweeteners or sugar

CHAPTER 9

CHRONIC DISEASES

1. **Free Radicals**
   a. Free radicals are atoms or groups of atoms that are highly reactive with other substances due to the fact that they have at least one unpaired electron. This causes them to bond with other compounds and cause damage to a wide variety of tissues in the body.
   b. Free radicals can attack cells and cell groups and play a role in chronic degenerative disease.
   c. Pollution, chemicals, drugs, stress and aging all produce free radicals primarily through the action of oxygen.
   d. The body has natural defenses to free radical damage. Antioxidants attack free radicals and protect membranes, nucleic acids and other cellular constituents from destruction.
   e. The antioxidant system is dependent upon nutrients such as vitamins E, C and A, beta carotene, selenium, zinc and others.
   f. Science has discovered powerful free radical fighters with greater protection potential than those previously known, including grape seed extract and CoEnzyme Q10.
   g. Lycopene, found in tomatoes and tomato sauce, has been found to be ten times more powerful than beta carotene.

2. **Hyperinsulinemia**
   • Production of too much insulin caused by elevated blood sugar
   Some of the consequences of hyperinsulinemia may be:
   a. Type II Diabetes
      • A loss of cellular sensitivity resulting in the need for greater and greater insulin production to maintain safe blood glucose levels. The resulting condition is adult-onset diabetes when the body is no longer able to sustain a higher production of insulin.
   b. Heart Disease
      • Insulin is a growth hormone which can cause muscle cells in the arterial walls to grow and narrow the vessels, contributing to atherosclerosis.
   c. Hypertension (High Blood Pressure)
      • Insulin causes the kidney to retain fluids, which increases blood volume.
   d. Obesity
      • Insulin facilitates the storage of energy in the fat cells.

3. **Osteoporosis**
   • Characterized by reduced bone mass and increased susceptibility to fractures

- Resistance exercise (strength training) stimulates the body to protect and increase bone density
4 **Type II Diabetes**
   - Characterized by reduced insulin secretion and/or reduced sensitivity to insulin
5. **Arthritis**
   - Osteoarthritis is characterized by deterioration of the joint.
   - Rheumatoid arthritis is characterized by bouts of swelling within the joint and is more common in women.
6. **Hypertension**
   - Chronically elevated high blood pressures greater than 140/90.
7. **Heart Disease**
   - The arteries that supply blood to the heart can narrow, calcify and ultimately cause a heart attack.

CHAPTER 10

PSYCHOLOGY OF CHANGE

1. **What's New**
   a. **The past need not predict the future.** We now know that strength training protects and prioritizes muscle tissue while we are trying to lose weight, and increases the body's energy requirements.
   b. **Plateaus.** As your body accesses stored energy due to actual starvation, a survival mechanism kicks in and hormones are produced which allow your body to operate more efficiently. But when we are trying to burn stored body fat, this hormonal response becomes a great disadvantage.
   c. **Perpetual dieting lowers metabolism.** Past dieting methods required that we diet forever to maintain weight loss because we did not have a means to raise metabolism without regaining weight.
   d. **Increase your metabolism.** The Phase III plan allows us to raise our metabolism to pre-diet levels without regaining weight, and ensures that we are able to maintain weight loss or lose more weight on Phases I and II.
2. **Embracing Change**
   a. People change due to one of three reasons:
      - They have spent adequate time in despair and frustration with their lives or circumstances
      - They have hit rock bottom
      - They learn that they can change

b. A rational plan provides a much better foundation for your efforts to change.
c. Motivation increases and becomes more reliable as you learn that you can change.
d. Change involves moving out of your comfort zone.
e. The conscious mind is the part of your mind that you are aware of. It is very limited in its capacity for storage or thought.
f. The subconscious mind has extraordinary capacity for storage and thought and makes the vast majority of our decisions.
g. You will program your subconscious mind to the point that you are successful in making good exercise and nutrition choices every day.
h. We are different from all other creatures in that we can choose to change our behaviors. The choice is made in our conscious mind. Most of it, however, is carried out though the subconscious mind via habits.

3. **Habits**
    a. It takes approximately 1 month to acquire a habit— good or bad.
    b. To develop a habit the following must happen:
        • You must have a goal.
        • A difficult goal requires perseverance.
        • Change will require a support group and an environment for change.

4. **Self-labels**
    a. We label ourselves based on early recordings and then we make many of our decisions based on often erroneous information.
    b. We often engage in behaviors that are not rational or helpful, and we do this because there is some payoff. We seek comfort rather than those things that might be best for us.

5. **Self-talk**
    a. We engage in self-dialogue on a continual basis.
    b. Self-talk is an extremely influential factor in our lives.
    c. Self-talk is a habit that can be changed.
    d. Self-talk that is helpful and accurate will reinforce the labels and life scripts that you choose.

6. **Environment**
    a. People become like those who surround them.
    b. Camaraderie of other women who share your goals is a great asset.
    c. Tell everyone what you are doing—this will increase motivation and accountability.
    d. Creating an environment for success requires a thousand deliberate choices made and remade every day.

7. **Attitude**
    a. Attitude is the state of mind through which you filter all information and make all decisions.
    b. We can choose our own attitude and determine our own quality of life.
    c. Attitude is a product of our character, self-labeling, self-talk, habits and environment.
    d. Helpful and accurate self-talk will reassure you of your value and purpose on a moment-to-moment basis.

8. **Goals**
    a. Goals must be specific and achievable.
    b. Goals must be written down.
    c. Set goals that will be motivating as well as reasonable.

9. **Enjoy the journey**
    a. Great things take time and involve many small steps rather than a few large steps.

10. **Obstacles**
    a. Any significant achievement will have times of failure.
    b. You may not arrive as quickly and efficiently as you desire, but you will arrive.
    c. Don't confuse disappointment with disaster.

11. **Be your own best friend.**
    a. Don't wait for others to encourage and motivate you.
    b. Value yourself enough to do it yourself.

FREE FOODS

You may have as much of these vegetables as you like. The closer to raw that you eat them, the better. Their calorie and carbohydrate content is subtracted from your daily totals.

green leafy vegetables
cabbage
celery
cucumbers
garlic
non-sweet onions
mushrooms
peppers
dill pickles
radishes
summer squash
zucchini

~

Curves shake made with
8 ounces of skim milk (one per day)

~

Flavoring choices:
yellow mustard
lemon juice

FREE FOODS SALAD

Any time salad is listed in your meal plan, use as much as you like of the free foods (see page 27 for a list of free foods). Add any of the following items according to your tastes and how many carbohydrates and calories you want to have. Use the blank lines to record your favorite salad additions.

FOOD ITEM	AMOUNT	CARBOHYDRATES	CALORIES
Artichoke hearts, water packed	3 pcs.	3 grams	18
Avocado	1/2	6 grams	162
Blue cheese, crumbled	1 Tbsp.	0 grams	30
Carrots	1/2 cup	6 grams	24
Egg, hard boiled	1	1 gram	75
Olives, black, sliced	1 Tbsp.	1 gram	9
Tomato	1 small	6 grams	30
Soy nuts, honey-roasted	1 Tbsp.	3 grams	29
Sunflower seed kernels	1 Tbsp.	1 gram	47

Don't forget the dressing—use something you like. Remember that fat free dressings often have more carbohydrates than the regular ones. (See page 29 for a Salad Dressing Table)

SALAD DRESSINGS

There is a dizzying array of salad dressings at most super-markets. In general, you want to find a salad dressing with few carbohydrates and limited calories. It must also taste good enough for you to enjoy it. Can you find a salad dressing with less than 4 carbohydrates and less than 50 calories in a serving of 2 tablespoons?

Record your favorites in the table below.

BRAND	KIND	PER 2 TABLESPOONS	
		CARBOHYDRATES	CALORIES

RESOURCES

BASIC KITCHEN TOOLS

kitchen scale
measuring cups
measuring spoons
colander

paring knife
utility knife
vegetable peeler
cutting board
grater

saucepan
sauté pan
skillet
broiler pan
meat thermometer
timer

can opener
mixing bowls
hand mixer
blender
whisk
wooden spoon

MEASUREMENT EQUIVALENTS

dash = less than $1/8$ teaspoon

3 teaspoons = 1 tablespoon

4 tablespoons = $1/4$ cup

$5^{1/3}$ tablespoons = $1/3$ cup

8 tablespoons = $1/2$ cup

$10^{2/3}$ tablespoons = $2/3$ cup

12 tablespoons = $3/4$ cup

14 tablespoons = $7/8$ cup

16 tablespoons = 1 cup

8 ounces = 1 cup

1 cup = $1/2$ pint

2 cups = 1 pint

16 ounces = 2 cups

2 pints (4 cups) = 1 quart

4 quarts (liquid) = 1 gallon

8 quarts (solid) = 1 peck

4 pecks = 1 bushel

16 ounces = 1 pound

Curves safety tip:
Ground beef patties and loaves are safe when they reach 160° F in the center; ground poultry patties and loaves are safe at 165° F.

PANTRY ESSENTIALS

chopped garlic (in a jar)
lemon juice
lemon pepper seasoning
light mayonnaise
olive oil
prepared yellow mustard
salad dressing
Curves shake mix

BASIC COOKING TERMS

Bake – To cook covered or uncovered in an oven or oven-type appliance. For meats cooked uncovered, it's called roasting.

Baste – To moisten foods during cooking with pan drippings or special sauce to add flavor and prevent drying.

Beat – To make mixture smooth by adding air with a brisk whipping or stirring motion using spoon, whisk or electric mixer.

Blend – To thoroughly mix two or more ingredients until smooth and uniform.

Boil – To cook in liquid at boiling temperature (212 degrees at sea level) where bubbles rise to the surface and break. For a full rolling boil, bubbles form rapidly throughout mixture.

Braise – To cook slowly with a small amount of liquid in tightly covered pan on top of range or in oven.

Broil – To cook by direct heat, usually under broiler in oven with door partially open or over coals.

Chop – To cut in pieces about the size of peas with knife, chopper or blender.

Cool – To remove from heat and let stand at room temperature.

Cream – To beat with spoon or electric mixer until mixture is soft and smooth. When applied to blending shortening and sugar, mixture is beaten until light and fluffy.

Cut in – To mix shortening with dry ingredients using pastry blender or knives.

Dice – To cut food in small cubes of uniform size and shape.

Glaze – A mixture applied to food which hardens or becomes firm and adds flavor and a glossy appearance.

Grill – An outdoor or indoor cooking method in which food is placed on a metal grid directly over a heat source, whether charcoal, wood, gas or electric coil. It also refers to cooking on a hot, flat metal surface.

Julienne – To cut food into long, thin strips.

Marinate – To allow food to stand in a liquid to tenderize or add flavor.

Mince – To cut or finely chop food into very small pieces.

Poach – To cook in hot liquid, being careful that food holds its shape.

Precook – To cook food partially or completely before final cooking or reheating.

Roast – To cook uncovered without water added, usually in an oven

Sauté – To brown or cook in small amount of butter or oil.

Steam – To cook in steam with or without pressure. A small amount of boiling water is used, and more water being added during steaming process if necessary.

Toss – To mix ingredients lightly.

Truss – To secure fowl or other meat with skewers during cooking.

Whip – To beat rapidly to incorporate air to produce expansion, usually in heavy cream or egg whites.

BASIC SPICES

Beef:
basil
chili powder
cumin
coriander
cilantro
oregano
parsley flakes
rosemary
sage
tarragon

Pork:
basil
chili powder
cumin
coriander
cilantro
oregano
parsley flakes
rosemary
sage

Lamb:
cumin
coriander
cilantro
oregano
rosemary
saffron

Chicken:
basil
chili powder
cumin
coriander
cilantro
ground mustard
oregano
parsley flakes
poultry season-
ing
rosemary
saffron
sage
tarragon

Turkey:
basil
chili powder
cumin
coriander
cilantro
oregano
parsley flakes
rosemary
sage
tarragon

Seafood:
basil
chili powder
cumin
coriander
cilantro
lemon pepper
oregano
rosemary
saffron
sage
tarragon

Shellfish:
basil
chili powder
cumin
coriander
cilantro
lemon pepper
paprika
parsley flakes
rosemary
tarragon

HOW TO COOK MEAT AND FISH

To cook meat and fish without adding fat and calories, grilling and broiling are good choices. Season meat or fish to your taste (be adventurous with spices) and grill or broil to desired doneness. Fish is fully cooked when it becomes opaque and flakes easily. Marinades can add delicious flavor to your meat or fish while adding minimal carbohydrates and calories. Check them out at your supermarket.

Fish may be baked in the oven at 375°F, but be sure to add some liquid and cover your baking dish. This will keep it moist. Good liquids to add are: chicken broth, lemon juice, wine or Italian dressing.

Meats and fish always taste great sautéed. You may use one tablespoon of olive oil or a nonstick spray in the sauté pan. Season meat or fish and cook to the desired doneness.

Chicken, pork and beef can be nicely cooked in a crock pot with some added liquid. The final result will be very tender and flavorful.

Experiment with these cooking methods to find your favorite.

DIETING ON THE GO

If you are working outside your home, this diet presents some challenges. You need to be able to take food with you and eat it at appropriate times.

Use your imagination about switching around the order of your meals. You might want to eat a meal in the morning and make a shake to take and drink later. Many of the meals are very portable and don't even require heating up. If you have access to a microwave oven, you have more options.

You will need a number of small containers and access to either a refrigerator or a small cooler. To take a salad, mix the leafy ingredients in one container and the wet ingredients (such as cucumber, tomato, etc.) in another. You can pack a measured amount of dressing in a very small container.

The key to making this diet work is planning.

FEEDING YOUR FAMILY
WHILE YOU FOLLOW
THE CURVES PLAN

On a daily basis, it is much too complicated to cook different meals for your family and yourself. The Curves Weight Loss Method meals are great for your family dinners. You may want to add a starch to the meal, such as rice, pasta, potatoes, grits or dressing. Another good addition to the meal is fruit. Of course, you need to not eat the starch nor the fruit in order to keep following the diet plan.

If you have trouble finding the will power to resist the foods that are not on your diet plan, it may help to fill the plates in the kitchen so that the serving dishes are not on the table while you eat.

Your family will probably love to have a chance to support your dieting efforts and everyone may gain some good new eating habits.

TIPS FOR EATING OUT

Given the hectic pace of life and our need for convenience, the average American eats away from home in restaurants about 8 times per month. A study at Tufts University in Boston found that the more often people eat out, the fatter they become. Here are a few tips to help you balance the need for convenience and still maintain a healthy diet plan while eating out.

• **Control portion sizes.** Restaurants of all types give you more food than the normal portion to create the appearance of price value. To combat this, share an entree with a friend or box half and take it home for another meal. You don't have to clean your plate to get your money's worth.

• **Drink water with your meal** and cut calories and cost. The average glass of soda or sweetened tea has about 150 calories and 40 carbohydrates.

• **Avoid the "urge to splurge"** each time you eat out. If you only eat out once a month, dessert is a fine part of an overall healthy eating plan. But with most of us eating out twice a week or more, it becomes more important to pass on the high calorie, high fat and high sugar treats each time. If you really want a dessert, order one and share it with others in your party.

• **Get it on the side.** Dressing, gravy, and sauce on your meal can add a lot of carbs and calories. Order these on the side to better control the amount you eat.

• **Ask lots of questions** about your selection. How is it cooked? What is served with it? Choose meats that are steamed, grilled, baked or broiled instead of fried. Trim visible fat from meat or skin from poultry.

• **You can't go wrong** with plain grilled meat or fish and salad or free vegetables.

• **Eat slowly and talk more.**

SEVEN WAYS TO SIZE UP YOUR PORTIONS

1 3 ounces of meat is about the size and thickness of a deck of playing cards or an audiotape cassette.

2 A medium apple or peach is about the size of a tennis ball.

3 1 ounce of cheese is about the size of 4 stacked dice.

4 ½ cup of ice cream is about the size of a racquetball or tennis ball.

5 1 cup of broccoli or mashed potatoes is about the size of your fist.

6 1 teaspoon of butter or peanut butter is about the size of the tip of your thumb.

7 1 ounce of nuts or small candies equals one handful.

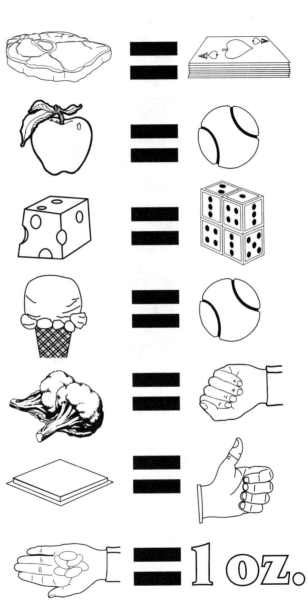

HOW TO READ
A NUTRITION LABEL

The food label can be found on food packages in your supermarket. Reading the label tells more about the food and what you are getting. What you see on the food label—the nutritional information and ingredient list—is required by the government.

Serving Size: Similar food products now have similar serving sizes. This makes it easier to compare foods.

Calories listed are per individual serving.

Vitamins and minerals: Only two vitamins, A and C, and two minerals, calcium and iron, are required on the food label. A food company can voluntarily list other vitamins and minerals in the food.

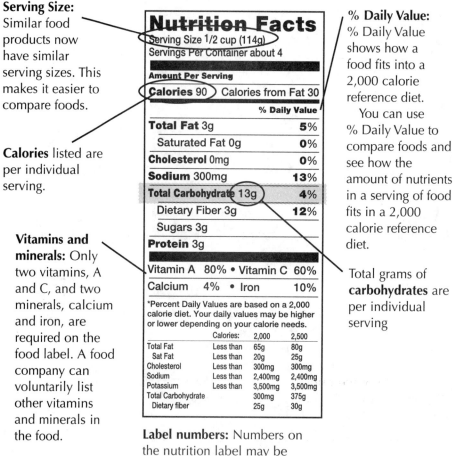

Nutrition Facts	
Serving Size 1/2 cup (114g)	
Servings Per Container about 4	

Amount Per Serving

Calories 90	Calories from Fat 30

	% Daily Value
Total Fat 3g	5%
Saturated Fat 0g	0%
Cholesterol 0mg	0%
Sodium 300mg	13%
Total Carbohydrate 13g	4%
Dietary Fiber 3g	12%
Sugars 3g	
Protein 3g	

Vitamin A 80% • Vitamin C 60%
Calcium 4% • Iron 10%

*Percent Daily Values are based on a 2,000 calorie diet. Your daily values may be higher or lower depending on your calorie needs.

	Calories:	2,000	2,500
Total Fat	Less than	65g	80g
Sat Fat	Less than	20g	25g
Cholesterol	Less than	300mg	300mg
Sodium	Less than	2,400mg	2,400mg
Potassium	Less than	3,500mg	3,500mg
Total Carbohydrate		300mg	375g
Dietary fiber		25g	30g

% Daily Value: % Daily Value shows how a food fits into a 2,000 calorie reference diet.

You can use % Daily Value to compare foods and see how the amount of nutrients in a serving of food fits in a 2,000 calorie reference diet.

Total grams of **carbohydrates** are per individual serving

Label numbers: Numbers on the nutrition label may be rounded for labeling.

Approximate number of calories per gram:

Fat – 9   Carbohydrate – 4   Protein – 4   Alcohol – 7

CURVES SHAKE VARIATIONS

The prescribed way to make the shake is with 8-ounces of skim milk (and 4 or 5 ice cubes, if you like it frosty and slushy). The Curves Shake comes in chocolate and vanilla flavors. Here are some different ways to make the shake and the changes to your carbohydrate and calorie counts.

- Use 8 ounces of 1% milk (tastes a little creamier)
  Add 0 carbohydrates and 30 calories.
- Use 8 ounces of 2% milk (tastes much creamier)
  Add 0 carbohydrates and 40 calories
- Use 8 ounces of whole milk (tastes rich and creamy)
  Add 0 carbohydrates and 70 calories
- Add 1 teaspoon real vanilla extract
  Add 1 carbohydrate and 10 calories
- Add $1/8$ to $1/4$ teaspoon mint extract
  Add 0 carbohydrate and 5 calories
- Add $1/4$ to $1/2$ teaspoon orange extract
  Add 0 carbohydrate and 11 calories
- Add $1/2$ teaspoon pure almond extract
  Add 0 carbohydrates and 11 calories
- Add 1 tablespoon coffee liquor
  Add 8 carbohydrates and 58 calories
- Add 1 tablespoon brandy
  Add 0 carbohydrates and 32 calories
- Instead of ice cubes, add $1/2$ of a frozen banana and whip up in a blender.
  Add 13 carbohydrates and 53 calories
- Add any fruit from another meal in the same day.

Use your imagination—you'll be surprised at the delicious combinations you can make up.

GUIDE TO FOOD DIARY ICONS

Mark out or fill in each icon as you complete it.

Water: 🥛 —each glass represents one 8-ounce glass of water consumed

Vitamins: ⬭ —each capsule is a reminder to take vitamin supplements

Daily Exercise: ♡ —check off your workout for the day: either the Curves Workout or something else such as walking, biking, pilates, dance, stretching, etc. Write down the type of exercise and how long you did the exercise.

HOW TO USE THE FOOD DIARY PAGES IN THE PERMANENT RESULTS WITHOUT PERMANENT DIETING WORKBOOK

Each day of this diet has its own food diary page on which your meals are laid out for you. Feel free to eat the meals in any order that works for you. It is very important to eat all six meals every day, which means that you will be eating every three or four hours. If you make a substitution, cross out what you did not eat and write in what you did eat. Check off the foods you do eat. Be sure to record the carbs and calories for the food you ate. Be sure to record everything you add to your Free Foods Salads, including dressing. Some foods have recipes provided in this book. At the top corner of the recipe page you can find the carbs and calories from free foods in the recipe. Make a note to subtract these along with your other free foods. You can circle or highlight the free foods so that it will be easy to add them up at the end of the day.

Record your water consumption by crossing out the water glass icons at the bottom of each food diary. You may want to use the vitamin pill icons to remind yourself to take vitamins and supplements. Record your exercise for the day.

At the end of the day, total up your carbs and calories. Then total up your free foods and subtract them to get your net totals for the day. A sample completed food diary page can be found opposite this page.

One of the most common reasons women are not successful on this diet is that they don't eat enough calories. If you are regularly below 1000 net calories, you must eat more calories without exceeding your carb limit.

Day: <u>Sample Food Diary Example</u>

			Carbs	Calories
Meal 1	✔	Curves shake with 8 oz. skim milk	(20)	(200)
Meal 2	✔	¹/₂ cup 1% fat cottage cheese	5	80
		~~¹/₂ cup strawberries~~	~~6~~	~~23~~
		1 peach	9	37
Meal 3	✔	4 ounces 93% lean ground beef, broiled	0	160
	✔	Free Foods Salad		
		¹/₂ avocado	6	162
		1 T. Blue Cheese	0	30
		¹/₂ tomato	3	47
		1 T. sunflower seeds	1	47
		2 T. Ranch dressing	1	140
Meal 4	✔	²/₃ cup tuna salad	4	264
	✔	*2 Rye Krisp crackers	11	60
			(-1)	(-6)
Meal 5	✔	4 ounces chicken breast, broiled	0	124
	✔	Parmesan Vegetable Stir Fry	22	275
			(-22)	(-100)
Meal 6	✔	3 ounces lean ham	0	100
	✔	*1 small apple	20	80
		1 dill pickle	(3)	(12)

	Carbs	Calories
Subtotals	102	1806
Minus Free Foods	-46	-318
Totals for Day	56	1488

Water: ▨▨▨▨▨▨▨▨

Vitamins: ⊘ ⊘ ⊘

Today's Exercise:

Curves Workout ⊘

or

Aerobic ♡

_____

_____

Strength Training ♡

_____

_____

Stretching ♡

_____

_____

If you are following the carbohydrate-restricted version, don't eat the foods that are marked with an asterisk (*). You are allowed to eat unlimited quantities of no-carb foods and free foods.

SUBSTITUTIONS

3 ounces tofu	=	1 egg
	=	3 ounces deli turkey
	=	3 ounces deli chicken
strawberries	=	blueberries
	=	raspberries
3 sausage links	=	5 ounces lean ham
4 ounces salmon	=	8 ounces orange roughy
plain lowfat yogurt	=	1% fat cottage cheese
2 Rye Krisp crackers	=	2 Harvest Multigrain crackers
Broccoli	=	Cauliflower
1 ounce Havarti cheese	=	1 ounce Cheddar cheese
$\frac{1}{2}$ cup cantaloupe	=	$\frac{1}{2}$ cup watermelon
	=	$\frac{1}{4}$ cup seedless grapes

Figure out some of your own substitutions.

_____ = _____

_____ = _____

_____ = _____

YOUR PERSONAL
FOOD DIRECTORY

It has been said that most people eat fewer than 15 foods on a regular basis. One of the keys to good nutrition is variety, so it is important to work at incorporating more and different foods into your regular diet.

A great tool for developing your own personal healthy eating plan is a Personal Food Directory with nutritional information for each food you regularly eat. Most people find it helpful to divide their Directory into types of foods such as: dairy products, fats, fruits, starches, protein, nuts, vegetables, prepared foods and other. Within each type, alphabetizing your list can make looking up the nutritional information more efficient. At a minimum, you will want to list serving size, calories and carbohydrates for each food entry. You may also want to know the protein, fat, fiber, cholesterol and sodium content of the foods.

Your best source of nutritional information is the package the food comes in. If there is no information on the package, you should be able to look the food up in a book such as *The Complete Book of Food Counts*, by Corinne T. Netzer.

There are also some computer programs that can assist you in making your Personal Food Directory.

The next 7 pages (pages 42-48) contain categorized lists of some common foods. Add your favorites at the bottom of each list, or write them on the chart on page 49.

This information is vital to your ability to make good food choices.

VEGETABLES

	amount	grams of carbohydrate	calories
Artichoke hearts, water packed	3 pieces	3	18
Asparagus, sliced	1/2 cup	4	22
Avocado	1/2 of medium	6	162
Broccoli florets	1 cup	5	24
*Cabbage, shredded	1 cup	4	16
Carrots, sliced	1 cup	11	48
Cauliflower florets	1 cup	5	26
*Celery	1/2 stalk	1	3
Corn (baby)	1/4 cup	2	15
Corn (whole kernel)	1/2 cup	13	66
*Cucumber, sliced	1/8 of medium	1	5
*Garlic	1 clove	1	4
Green beans, cut	1/2 cup	4	20
*Green Onion	1 piece	0	1
*Green onion, sliced	1 tablespoon	1	4
*Lettuce leaves	4 large	3	12
*Lettuce leaves, torn up	2 cups	4	16
*Mushrooms, sliced	1/2 cup	4	21
Olives, ripe, sliced	1/2 cup	1	9
*Onion	1/2 of medium	14	60
*Onion, chopped	1 cup	14	60
Peas, green	1/2 cup	11	60
*Pepper, green & red bell	1 medium	5	20
*Pickles, dill	1 medium	3	12
Pickles, sweet	1 medium	10	41
*Radishes	1 piece	0	1
*Sauerkraut	1/2 cup	5	20
Snow peas	1/2 cup	7	30
*Spinach, fresh	1 cup (packed)	2	12
*Summer Squash, sliced	1/2 cup	3	13
Tomato	1/2 of medium	3	15
Tomato paste	1 tablespoon	3	12
V-8 juice	1 cup (8 ounce)	10	46
*Zucchini, sliced	1/2 cup	2	9

*Free Foods

FRUITS

	amount	grams of carbohydrate	calories
Apple, with peel	1 small	20	80
Banana	$1/2$ of medium	13	53
Blueberries	$1/4$ cup	7	27
Cantaloupe, cubed	$1/2$ cup	6	25
Cranberries, dried & sweetened	$1/3$ cup	33	130
Grapefruit	$1/2$ of medium	12	46
Grapes, seedless	$1/2$ cup	14	57
Lime juice	$1 1/2$ tablespoons	1	5
Nectarine	1 medium	16	67
Orange	1 medium	16	65
Orange juice	$2 1/2$ tablespoons	4	17
Orange juice, from concentrate	1 cup (8 ounce)	28	110
Peach, peeled	1 medium	9	37
Plum	1 medium	9	36
Raspberries	$1/4$ cup	4	17
Strawberries	$1/2$ cup	6	23
Watermelon, cubed	$1/2$ cup	6	25

PROTEIN

	grams of carbohydrate	calories
Poultry		
4 oz. chicken breast, grilled or broiled	0	124
4 oz. fajita chicken	0	120
4 oz. turkey breast, grilled or broiled	0	120
4 oz. deli turkey breast	4	120
Beef		
4 oz. broiled sirloin	0	215
4 oz. roast beef, deli	4	120
1/4 lb. hamburger patty (93% lean)	0	160
1/4 lb. hamburger patty (96% lean)	0	130
Pork		
4 oz. center cut pork chop, lean, broiled	0	150
4 oz. pork loin	0	150
3 oz lean ham	0	100
4 oz. light smoked sausage	8	220
Fish		
6 oz. tuna, packed in water	0	180
4 oz. salmon, broiled	0	207
4 oz. rainbow trout	0	200
1/4 lb. shrimp, broiled or grilled	0	120
8 oz. orange roughy	0	216
Eggs		
large	1	75
Tofu		
3 oz. tofu (extra firm)	1	90

NUTS

	amount	grams of carbohydrate	calories
Almonds, roasted & salted	1 ounce	4	180
Cashews, roasted & salted	1 ounce	7	170
Macadamia nuts, roasted & salted	1 ounce	3	220
Peanuts, dry roasted	1 ounce	5	160
Pistachio nuts, in shells	2 ounces	7	170
Soy nuts, honey roasted	2 tablespoons	5	58
Sunflower seed kernels, roasted & salted	1 tablespoon	1	47

FATS

	amount	grams of carbohydrate	calories
Butter	1 tablespoon	0	102
Mayonnaise	1 tablespoon	0	100
Mayonnaise, light	1 tablespoon	1	50
Oil, olive	1 tablespoon	0	120
Oil, other	1 tablespoon	0	120

GRAINS AND STARCHES

	amount	grams of carbohydrate	calories
Cornstarch	1 tablespoon	7	30
Flour, all-purpose	1 tablespoon	7	28
Refried beans, traditional	1/2 cup	25	120
Holland Rusk Dry Toast	1 piece	6	30
Pepperidge Farm light bread	1 slice	9	45
Whole wheat bread	1 slice	12	70
All Bran Cereal	2 tablespoons	6	20
Oatmeal, cooked (Old Fashioned)	1 cup	27	150
Crackers, Rye Krisp	2 crackers	11	60
Harvest Bakery Multigrain Crackers	2 crackers	11	70

MISCELLANEOUS

	amount	grams of carbohydrate	calories
Beef broth, canned	1 cup	0	18
Chicken broth, canned	1 cup	1	30
Chocolate chips	1/2 cup	52	440
Chocolate syrup	2 tablespoons	24	100
Chocolate, unsweetened	1 ounce	4	95
Ice cream, chocolate	1/2 cup	19	160
Ice cream, French vanilla	1/2 cup	15	160
Brandy	1/2 cup	0	296
Sherry, dry	1 tablespoon	0	15
Wine, red	1/4 cup	0	44
Wine, white or rosé	1/2 cup	6	100
Barbeque sauce	1 tablespoon	6	25
Heinz 57 sauce	1 tablespoon	5	18
Salsa	2 tablespoons	2	10
Soy sauce	1 tablespoon	1	10
Tabasco sauce	1/4 teaspoon	0	0
Wine vinegar	1 tablespoon	1	2
Worcestershire sauce	1 teaspoon	1	5
Yellow mustard	1/2 tablespoon	0	1
Brown sugar, packed	1 tablespoon	13	51
Sugar	1 tablespoon	12	46

DAIRY PRODUCTS

	amount	grams of carbohydrate	calories
Blue cheese, crumbled	1 tablespoon	0	30
Cheddar cheese	1 ounce	0	110
Feta cheese, reduced fat, crumbled	1 tablespoon	0	15
Havarti cheese	1 ounce	0	120
Monterey Jack cheese	1 ounce	0	110
Parmesan cheese, shredded	2 tablespoons	0	55
Pepper Jack cheese	1 ounce	1	110
Swiss cheese	1 ounce	0	110
Cottage cheese, 1% fat	$1/2$ cup	5	80
Cottage cheese, 2% fat	$1/2$ cup	5	90
Cream cheese	2 tablespoons	1	100
Cream cheese, light	2 tablespoons	1	74
Cream cheese, vegetable	2 tablespoons	2	90
Cream, whipping	1 tablespoon	0	52
Milk, 2% fat	8 ounces	12	120
Milk, skim	8 ounces	12	84
Milk, whole	8 ounces	12	150
Yogurt, plain, lowfat	8 ounces	18	150

CHEESE

	grams of carbohydrate	calories
Soft Cheeses		
Brie, 1 oz.	0	95
Camembert, 1oz.	0	85
Ricotta, 1/4 cup	3	110
Cottage, 1% fat, 1/2 cup	5	80
Cream, 2 tablespoons	1	100
Semi-Soft Cheeses		
Blue, crumbled, 1 oz. (2 tablespoons)	0	60
Brick, 1 oz.	0	110
Feta, 1 oz.	0	80
Havarti, 1 oz.	0	120
Monterey Jack, 1 oz.	0	110
Mozzarella, part skim, 1 oz.	1	80
Muenster, 1 oz.	0	100
Provolone, 1 oz.	0	100
Hard Cheeses		
Cheddar, 1 oz.	0	110
Colby, 1 oz.	0	110
Edam, 1 oz.	0	90
Gouda, 1 oz.	0	110
Swiss, 1 oz.	0	110
Very Hard Cheese		
Parmesan, grated, 1 tablespoon	0	28
Parmesan, shredded, 1/4 cup	0	110
Romano, grated, 1 tablespoon	0	28
Other		
American, Pasteurized Process, 3/4 oz. slice	0	80

MY FAVORITES

	amount	grams of carbohydrate	calories

VITAMINS

Vitamin	Function	Food Sources
Vitamin A (Retinol, Beta Carotene)	• growth and repair of body tissue and immune functions • night vision * *toxic in doses of 25,000 or more International Units a day)*	liver, cream, butter, whole milk, egg yolk, green and yellow vegetables, yellow fruits, fortified margarine
Vitamin D (Cholecalciferol)	• calcium and phosphorus metabolism (bone & teeth formation)	fortified milk, fortified margarine, fish oils, sunlight on skin
Vitamin E (Tocopherol)	• protects cell membranes and red blood cells from oxidation • may be active in immune function	vegetable oils
Vitamin K	• formation of blood clotting agents • *toxicity can be induced by water soluble analogs*	cheese, egg yolk, liver, green leafy vegetables, also synthesized by intestinal bacteria
B1 (Thiamin)	• carbohydrate metabolism • appetite maintenance • nerve function • growth and muscle tone	pork, beef, liver, whole or enriched grains, legumes
B2 (Riboflavin)	• carbohydrate, fat and protein metabolism • needed for cell respiration • mucous membranes * *toxic in doses above 100 milligrams a day*	milk, liver, enriched cereals
Niacin	• carbohydrate, fat and protein metabolism • health of digestive system, blood circulation, nerve functioning * *toxic in slow-released doses of 500 mg or more a day or immediate-release doses of 750 mg or more a day)*	meat, peanuts, enriched grains
Vitamin B6 (Pyridoxine)	• carbohydrate and protein metabolism • formation of antibodies • red blood cells • nerve function	wheat, corn, meat, liver
Folate (folic acid)	• red blood cell formation • protein metabolism • cell growth and division	liver, green leafy vegetables
Vitamin C (Ascorbic Acid)	• aids wound healing, strengthens blood vessels, collagen maintenance, resistance to infection, healthy gums	citrus fruits, berries, mangos, papayas, melons, tomatoes, potatoes, green peppers and leafy green vegetables

Sources: National Academy Press, American Society for Nutritional Sciences

MINERALS

Mineral	Function	Food Sources
Calcium	• support of bones, teeth, muscle tissue • regulates heartbeat • muscle action • nerve function • blood clotting	dairy, fish (with bones), tofu, legumes, kale, broccoli, fortified foods
Chromium	• needed for glucose metabolism(energy) • increases effectiveness of insulin • muscle function	fruits, vegetables, vegetable oils, whole grains, seeds, brewer's yeast
Copper	• formation of red blood cells, pigment • needed for bone health	meat, drinking water
Iodine	• function of thyroid gland, which controls metabolism	iodized salt, bread, seafood
Iron	• formation of hemoglobin in blood and myoglobin in muscle, which supply oxygen to cells	beef, fish, poultry, shellfish, eggs, legumes, dried fruits, fortified cereals
Magnesium	• enzyme activation • nerve and muscle function • bone growth	legumes, whole grain cereals, nuts, dark green vegetables, chocolate, mineral water
Manganese	• bone growth and development • sex hormone production • cell function	non-animal sources only: fruits, vegetables, pecans, peanuts, fruit juice, oatmeal, rice
Phosphorus	• bone development • carbohydrate, fat and protein utilization	dairy, yogurt, fish, beef, poultry, eggs, legumes, grains
Potassium	• fluid balance • controls activity of heart muscle • nervous system	Fruit, vegetables, dairy, grains, legumes, beef
Selenium	• fights cell damage from oxidation	seafood, meats, grains, Brazil nuts
Sodium	• acid-base balance • fluid retention • involved in nerve impulse transmission	table salt, soy sauce, pickled foods, canned foods, many processed foods
Zinc	• taste and smell sensitivity • regulation of metabolism • aids in healing	beef, fish, poultry, grains, vegetables

Sources: National Academy Press, American Society for Nutritional Sciences

WATER

A woman's body is usually 50-55% water. Body water performs three essential functions:

1. helps give structure and form to the body by plumping up tissues,
2. creates the water-based environment necessary for the chemical actions and reactions that make up the body's metabolism and sustain life,
3. provides the means for maintaining a stable body temperature.
4. protects the kidneys and helps detoxify the body

Obviously, it is very important that we drink adequate water every day. Our health depends on it, and so does our beauty. Drinking plenty of water helps to maintain good skin tone and color. It is also of great assistance in maintaining normal digestion.

We all need to drink at least 8 (8-ounce) glasses of water every day. (2 quarts)

Caffeinated beverages act as a mild diuretic, and so they should not be counted as a part of your daily water intake.

FIBER

Fiber is a very important part of our diet. Eating plenty of fiber can have a positive impact on diabetes, heart disease, colon cancer and other gastrointestinal diseases.

The recommended daily allowance of dietary fiber is 20 to 35 grams per day (for adults). This goal can be easily achieved through generous consumption of whole grains, legumes, vegetables, fruits, seeds and nuts.

The Curves Weight Loss Method may have less fiber than you are accustomed to. If you are troubled by irregularity, cramps or other symptoms, you may want to consider supplementing your fiber intake. Powdered fiber can be added to your daily protein shake (about 1 teaspoon) or to yogurt. Your supermarket or pharmacy probably has a number of fiber supplement options. Finally, be sure to drink plenty of water to ease digestive symptoms.

A great way to increase your total fiber intake is to eat $1/4$ cup of a bran cereal (such as Fiber One) with $1/4$ cup skim milk (no sugar allowed!) Use the table below to record the carb, calorie, and fiber counts of some of the cereals you might try.

	amount	grams of carbohydrate	calories	fiber
skim milk	$1/4$ cup	3	21	0
Fiber One	$1/4$ cup	12	30	6.5
All Bran	$1/4$ cup	12	40	5.5

SPICY ZUCCHINI BOATS

Prep time: 20 minutes
Cook time: 12 minutes

4 small zucchini
Boiling, salted water

Stuffing:
4 ounces light cream cheese, softened
$1/2$ cup (2 ounces) shredded pepper jack cheese
$1/2$ cup shredded Parmesan cheese
$1/4$ teaspoon cayenne pepper
1 teaspoon dried chives

Preheat oven to 350 degrees. Slice zucchini in half lengthwise to make boats. Blanch zucchini in boiling, salted water, 2 minutes. Drain, then immediately immerse zucchini in an ice bath. Drain thoroughly; blot excess water with paper towels.

Using a knife or small spoon, carefully hollow out zucchini by removing some of its pulp. (Leave at least a $1/4$-inch wall.)

Combine cheeses, cayenne pepper and chives in mixing bowl. Stuff zucchini with cheese mixture. Place in lightly-greased baking dish. Bake until squash is heated through, and cheese is melted, 8 to 10 minutes.

Makes 4 (2-piece) servings.

● *(per serving) Calories 210, Carbohydrates 5 gm, Protein 13 gm, Fat 16 gm, Sat Fat 7 gm, Fiber 1 gm, Cholesterol 48 mg, Sodium 476 mg*

Curves Tip: *Cover leftovers and refrigerate; reheat in microwave another day.*

(This recipe's ingredients are not included in your shopping list.)

TURKEY-LETTUCE WRAPS

Prep time: 10 minutes

   8 *butter lettuce leaves*
 $1/2$ *cup vegetable cream cheese, softened*
 $1/2$ *cucumber, peeled and diced*
 $1/4$ *cup roasted and salted sunflower seeds*
   8 *($1/2$-ounce) slices deli turkey breast*

Spread each lettuce leaf with 1 tablespoon cream cheese. Evenly divide cucumber and sunflower seeds between lettuce leaves and sprinkle over the cream cheese. Top each lettuce leaf with 1 slice of turkey. Press down gently and roll up.

   Makes 8 wraps

🍎 *(per wrap) Calories 87, Carbohydrates 7 gm, Protein 5 gm, Fat 6 gm, Sat Fat 3 gm, Fiber 0 gm, Cholesterol 20 mg, Sodium 254 mg*

(This recipe's ingredients are not included in your shopping list.)

ITALIAN STUFFED MUSHROOMS

Prep time: 30 minutes

$^1/_4$ *pound bulk Italian sausage*

$^1/_2$ *cup onion, minced*

  2 *cloves garlic, minced*

$^1/_2$ *cup zucchini, shredded*

$^1/_2$ *teaspoon oregano*

$^1/_4$ *teaspoon thyme*

  1 *teaspoon dried parsley flakes*

$^1/_2$ *teaspoon salt*

  3 *Rye Krisp crackers, smashed into fine crumbs (approximately $^1/_4$ cup)*

  2 *tablespoons shredded Parmesan cheese*

  2 *tablespoons red wine*

  2 *tablespoons water*

18 *large button mushrooms, washed*

Spray skillet with cooking spray. Brown sausage, breaking up into small crumbles as it cooks. Add onion and cook until tender. Add garlic, zucchini and spices and cook well. Turn off heat under skillet. Add crumbs, cheese, wine and water, and mix well. Remove stems from mushrooms and discard. Stuff mushroom caps with filling, piling high. Place in glass dish and cover tightly with microwave safe plastic wrap. Microwave on high power 6 to 8 minutes. Let stand 5 to 7 minutes before serving.

Makes 3 servings. (6 mushrooms each)

🍎 *(per serving) Calories 192, Carbohydrates 16 gm, Protein 9 gm, Fat 9 gm, Sat Fat 3 gm, Fiber 4 gm, Cholesterol 24 mg, Sodium 734 mg*

(This recipe's ingredients are not included in your shopping list.)

TUNA SALAD

Prep time: 10 minutes

1 (6-ounce) can solid white Albacore tuna (water packed)
1 green onion, minced
$^1/_2$ stalk celery, minced
1 radish, minced or shredded
$^1/_2$ teaspoon lemon juice
$^1/_2$ teaspoon lemon pepper
$^1/_2$ tablespoon yellow mustard
$1^1/_2$ tablespoons light mayonnaise

Drain tuna and break up with a fork. Add remaining ingredients and mix well.

Makes $^2/_3$ cup (1 serving)

🍎 *(per serving) Calories 264, Carbohydrates 4 gm, Protein 34 gm, Fat 12.5 gm, Sat Fat 3.5 gm, Fiber 0 gm, Cholesterol 75 mg, Sodium 1309 mg*

Curves Tip: *Mix up enough tuna salad for the week at one time.*

SPINACH SALAD
WITH ORANGE VINAIGRETTE

Prep time: 15 minutes

Vinaigrette:
2$^1/_2$ tablespoons orange juice
    1 tablespoon wine vinegar
1$^1/_2$ tablespoons extra-virgin or virgin olive oil
  $^1/_4$ teaspoon pepper
  $^1/_2$ teaspoon salt (or to taste)

Salad:
    2 cups (lightly packed) fresh spinach or baby spinach
  $^1/_2$ cup sliced fresh mushrooms
  $^1/_2$ cup thinly sliced red onion

   For vinaigrette: Combine orange juice and vinegar in shaker.
Add oil, salt and pepper. Shake well.
   For salad: Place ingredients in a serving bowl. Toss with vinaigrette to
coat vegetables.
   Serve immediately.
   Makes 2 servings.

🍎 *(per serving) Calories 138, Carbohydrates 11 gm, Protein 2 gm, Fat 10 gm, Sat Fat 0 gm, Fiber 2 gm,
Cholesterol 0 mg, Sodium 577 mg*

(This recipe's ingredients are not included in your shopping list.)

GREEK SALAD

Prep time: 20 minutes
Marinating time: at least one hour

4 ounces cooked chicken breast (no skin or breading), sliced

Dressing:
 1^1/$_2$ tablespoons olive oil
 1^1/$_2$ tablespoons lemon juice
 1 clove garlic, mashed
 ^{1}/$_2$ teaspoon lemon pepper seasoning
 ^{1}/$_4$ teaspoon salt
 ^{1}/$_4$ teaspoon dried oregano
 ^{1}/$_4$ teaspoon dried basil

Salad:
 2 cups romaine lettuce or iceberg lettuce (or mixture)
 ^{1}/$_8$ cucumber, sliced
 ^{1}/$_2$ tomato, chopped
 ^{1}/$_8$ cup red onion, thinly sliced
 1 tablespoon sliced black olives
 1 tablespoon reduced-fat feta cheese, crumbled

Whisk together dressing ingredients and pour over cooked, sliced chicken breast. Marinate in refrigerator at least one hour. Make salad and toss with chicken and dressing.

Makes 1 serving.

🍎 *(per serving) Calories 383, Carbohydrates 14 gm, Protein 29 gm, Fat 24 gm, Sat Fat .5 gm, Fiber 2 gm, Cholesterol 64 mg, Sodium 949 mg*

(This recipe's ingredients are not included in your shopping list.)

CREAMY COLESLAW

Prep time: 10 minutes
Chilling time: 1 hour

Dressing:

2 tablespoons heavy cream

2 tablespoons light mayonnaise

1 tablespoon vinegar

$^1/_2$ tablespoon sugar

$^1/_2$ teaspoon salt

$^1/_2$ teaspoon celery seed

$^1/_4$ teaspoon black pepper

4 cups (packed) shredded cabbage (approximately 8 ounces)

Mix dressing ingredients well. Pour over cabbage and mix. Chill until cold (at least 1 hour). The mixture will pack down to about 1$^1/_2$ cups.
Makes 3 ($^1/_2$ cup) servings.

🍎 *(per serving) Calories 99, Carbohydrates 8 gm, Protein 0 gm, Fat 7 gm, Sat Fat 3 gm, Fiber 1 gm, Cholesterol 14 mg, Sodium 449 mg*

(This recipe's ingredients are not included in your shopping list.)

FRENCH ONION SOUP

Prep time: 1 hour
Cook time: 1 hour

4 tablespoons butter ($^1/_2$ stick)
4 cups onions, thinly sliced (2-3 onions)
2 cups sliced mushrooms
$1^1/_2$ tablespoons flour
6 cups beef broth (not bouillon)
$^1/_2$ teaspoon salt
$^1/_2$ teaspoon pepper
$^1/_2$ cup brandy
$^1/_2$ teaspoon Kitchen Bouquet seasoning

On the stovetop, in a soup pot, melt the butter and add the onions, stirring constantly. Cook for 15 to 20 minutes, or until soft.

When the onions are soft, add mushrooms, cook 2 minutes and sprinkle them with flour. Stir and add 2 cups of beef broth. Continue to stir until the mixture is thickened. Add the remaining broth, and stir in salt, pepper and brandy. Bring to a boil. Cover and simmer for 45 minutes. Add the Kitchen Bouquet, and then taste for seasonings and correct if necessary.

Makes 6 ($1^1/_3$ cup) servings.

🍎 *(Per serving): Calories 199, Carbohydrates 15 gm, Protein 4 gm, Fat 8.5 gm, Sat Fat 6 gm, Fiber 3 gm, Cholesterol 21 mg, Sodium 1735 mg*

Curves Note: *Divide up into single servings and freeze until you are ready to eat.*
Curves Tip: *This soup is delicious served with 1 tablespoon shredded Parmesan cheese sprinkled on top before serving.*

(This recipe's ingredients are not included in your shopping list.)

BEEF AND VEGETABLE STEW

Prep time: 30 minutes
Cook time: 7 to 9 hours in crockpot

2 pounds lean beef stew meat
1 tablespoon olive oil
1 onion, sliced thinly
1 green pepper, julienne sliced
6 celery stalks, sliced
4 cups baby carrots
3 cloves garlic, minced
1 cup V-8 juice
1 teaspoon Heinz 57 steak sauce
1 teaspoon Worcestershire sauce
$^1/_4$ cup red wine
$^1/_2$ cup beef broth
1 teaspoon dried parsley flakes
1 tablespoon cornstarch

Brown beef in olive oil. Place meat and drippings in a large crock pot. Place vegetables on top of meat. Mix liquid ingredients and parsley and pour into crock pot. Cook on high for 7 to 9 hours. One hour before serving, mix cornstarch with 1 tablespoon water, stir until smooth. Stir into stew and mix well.

Before serving, taste and adjust seasonings, if necessary.

Makes 8 servings.

🍎 *(per serving) Calories 280, Carbohydrates 13 gm, Protein 24 gm, Fat 14 gm, Sat Fat 5 gm, Fiber 3 gm, Cholesterol 60 mg, Sodium 251 mg*

Curves Tip: *Freeze unused stew in single servings for later use.*

(This recipe's ingredients are not included in your shopping list.)

BEEF TENDERLOIN
WITH BLUE CHEESE

Prep and marinating time: 1 hour
Cook time: 10 to 12 minutes

6 (6-ounce) pieces of tenderloin, 1 1/2 to 2 inches thick
(2 to 2 1/2 pounds, if buying whole tenderloin and slicing it yourself)

Marinade:
1 tablespoon olive oil
1/4 cup red wine
1 clove garlic, minced
1 tablespoon tomato paste
1 tablespoons chopped fresh parsley
(or 1 teaspoon dried parsley flakes)
Salt and freshly cracked pepper to taste

1/2 tablespoon blue cheese per serving

Mix marinade ingredients in a large baking dish. Coat both sides of meat with the marinade, and let filets sit in refrigerator for 30 to 45 minutes. Grill filets over medium-high heat, or broil 6 inches from heat source, until cooked. Medium doneness is recommended (160 degrees on a meat thermometer). Top with blue cheese and cook until melted.
Serves 6.

🍎 *(per serving) Calories 383, Carbohydrates 1 gm, Protein 38 gm, Fat 24 gm, Sat Fat 10 gm, Fiber 0 gm, Cholesterol 120 mg, Sodium 470 mg*

(This recipe's ingredients are not included in your shopping list.)

FREE FOODS
IN THIS RECIPE:
**mushrooms, onion,
spinach**
*take off 59 calories and
12 carbohydrates per serving*

EASY FRITTATA

Prep time: 15 minutes

$1/2$ pound 93% lean ground beef
1 tablespoon butter
2 cups sliced mushrooms
$1/2$ onion, chopped (approximately 1 cup)
2 teaspoons Worcestershire sauce
1 teaspoon dried oregano
$1/2$ teaspoon garlic powder
1 teaspoon salt
$1/4$ teaspoon black pepper
1 teaspoon dried parsley flakes
2 cups chopped fresh spinach
4 large eggs
$1/4$ cup skim milk
$1/2$ cup shredded Parmesan cheese

Spray large skillet with nonstick cooking spray. Add ground beef, butter, mushrooms and onion; cook over medium-high heat 6 to 8 minutes or until onion is tender, breaking beef apart with spoon. Add Worcestershire sauce and seasonings. Cook until meat is no longer pink.

Stir spinach into meat mixture. Push mixture to one side of pan. Reduce heat to medium. Beat eggs with skim milk and pour into other side of pan; cook, without stirring, 1 to 2 minutes or until set on bottom. Lift eggs to allow uncooked portion to flow underneath. Repeat until softly set. Gently stir into meat mixture and heat through. Stir in cheese.

Makes 3 servings.

🍎 *(per serving) Calories 384, Carbohydrates 16 gm, Protein 33 gm, Fat 21 gm, Sat Fat 10 gm, Fiber 4 gm, Cholesterol 356 mg, Sodium 1176 mg*

(This recipe's ingredients are not included in your shopping list.)

SPICY CHILI PORK CHOPS

Prep time: 25 minutes

 4 boneless pork chops (4 ounces each)

Rub:
 $^1/_2$ tablespoon salt
 $^1/_2$ tablespoon cumin
 $^1/_2$ tablespoon black pepper
 $^1/_2$ tablespoon chili powder
 1 tablespoon paprika
 $^1/_2$ tablespoon garlic powder
 $^1/_2$ tablespoon ground ginger

   Trim fat from pork chops. Mix spices together. Rub the spice mixture into all sides of meat. Broil or grill 10 to 15 minutes on each side or until done.
   Serves 4.

 🍎 *(per serving) Calories 219, Carbohydrates 4 gm, Protein 19 gm, Fat 14 gm, Sat Fat 2.5 gm, Fiber 0 gm, Cholesterol 2 mg, Sodium 1652 mg*

   (This recipe's ingredients are not included in your shopping list.)

SHERRY-MUSHROOM CHICKEN

Prep time: 45 minutes

3 (6 ounce) boneless, skinless chicken breasts
2 tablespoons olive oil
1$^1/_2$ cups chopped fresh mushrooms
2 tablespoons sliced green onion
1 clove garlic, minced
1 tablespoon cornstarch
1 tablespoon chopped fresh parsley or 1 teaspoon dried parsley flakes
$^1/_2$ teaspoon dried thyme
dash black pepper
$^2/_3$ cup chicken broth
1 tablespoon dry sherry

In a large skillet, sauté chicken breasts in olive oil for 15 minutes or until done. When cooked, remove and keep warm in the oven while you prepare the sauce. Sauté mushrooms, green onion and garlic in skillet over medium heat until tender. Stir in cornstarch, parsley, thyme and pepper. Stir in broth and sherry. Cook and stir until sauce boils and thickens. Serve sauce over chicken.

Makes 3 servings.

🍎 *(per serving) Calories 314, Carbohydrates 8 gm, Protein 43 gm, Fat 11.5 gm, Sat Fat 1 gm, Fiber 1 gm, Cholesterol 96 gm, Sodium 113 mg*

(This recipe's ingredients are not included in your shopping list.)

JAMAICAN SEAFOOD MEDLEY

Prep time: 10 minutes
Marinating time: at least 2 hours
Cook time: 20 minutes

Marinade:
- 2 tablespoons packed brown sugar
- 1 1/2 tablespoons orange juice
- 1 1/2 tablespoons lime juice
- 2 cloves garlic, minced
- 1/2 teaspoon minced ginger
- 1 teaspoon grated orange peel
- 1 teaspoon grated lime peel
- 1 teaspoon salt
- 1/2 teaspoon black pepper
- 1/8 teaspoon ground cinnamon
- dash ground cloves
- 1/2 teaspoon Tabasco sauce

- 1/2 pound orange roughy, cut into bite-sized pieces
- 1/2 pound sea scallops, cut in half (or quarters, if very large)
- 1/2 pound shrimp, shelled and deveined
- 1 tablespoon olive oil
- 3/4 cup baby corn, snapped in fourths
- 1 tablespoon green onions, sliced
- 1/2 green pepper, julienne sliced

Combine sugar, juices and seasonings. Pour over seafood; mix well. Cover and refrigerate at least 2 hours. Drain seafood and discard marinade. Saute seafood and vegetables in olive oil over medium heat for 15 minutes or until done. Serves 3.

🍎 *(per serving) Calories 287, Carbohydrates 7 gm, Protein 41 gm, Fat 10.5 gm, Sat Fat 0.5 gm, Fiber 2 gm, Cholesterol 156 mg, Sodium 433 mg*

(This recipe's ingredients are not included in your shopping list.)

TOFU STIR-FRY

Prep time: 15 minutes

   3 ounces firm tofu (¹/₅ block)
   2 tablespoons olive oil
¹/₂ onion, thinly sliced
   1 clove garlic, chopped
¹/₂ cup mushrooms, sliced
¹/₂ cup zucchini, sliced
¹/₂ cup fresh spinach, packed
   1 tablespoon soy sauce
   1 tablespoon water

Press water from tofu by putting between several layers of paper towels and placing a dinner plate on top. Let sit 20 to 30 minutes. Divide block into 5 portions. (*The 4 unused portions of tofu may be frozen in individual bags for later use.*)

Cube tofu and stir fry in olive oil. Add onion and garlic and cook 3 to 4 minutes. Add mushrooms and cook until done. Add zucchini and cook a few minutes. Add spinach, soy sauce and water. Stir well and cook 1 to 2 minutes.

Serves 1.

🍎 *(Per serving): Calories 440, Carbohydrates 25 gm, Protein 12 gm, Fat 31.5 gm, Sat Fat 1 gm, Fiber 4 gm, Cholesterol 0 mg, Sodium 989 mg*

Curves Tip: *3 ounces of chicken can be substituted for tofu. (Nutritional information remains approximately the same.)*

FREE FOODS
IN THIS RECIPE:
**onion, garlic, lemon
juice mushrooms,
spinach**
*take off 100 calories and
22 carbohydrates per serving*

PARMESAN VEGETABLE STIR-FRY

Prep time: 15 minutes

1 tablespoon olive oil
$^{1}/_{2}$ onion, thinly sliced
1 clove garlic, chopped
$^{1}/_{2}$ cup mushrooms, sliced
1 cup fresh spinach
1 tablespoon lemon juice
$^{1}/_{2}$ ounce (2 tablespoons) Parmesan cheese, shredded

Sauté onion and garlic in olive oil until soft. Add mushrooms and cook until done. Add spinach, toss well and sauté very briefly. Sprinkle on lemon juice and Parmesan cheese. Serve hot.

Makes 1 serving.

🍎 *(per serving) Calories 275, Carbohydrates 22 gm, Protein 8 gm, Fat 17 gm, Sat Fat 0 gm, Fiber 6 gm, Cholesterol 10 mg, Sodium 1189 mg*

FROZEN CHOCOLATE MOUSSE

Prep time: 30 minutes
Freezing time: at least 1 hour

    12 ounces silken (soft) tofu
    $^1/_2$ cup semisweet chocolate chips
    $1^1/_2$ ounces unsweetened chocolate
    $^1/_2$ cup Splenda (granular)
    $^1/_4$ cup water
     3 egg whites
    $^1/_4$ teaspoon salt
     2 tablespoons heavy cream
     1 teaspoon vanilla extract

Remove tofu from water in package and place between several layers of paper towels. Weight with a plate for at least 15 minutes to press excess water out of tofu.

Place chocolate chips and unsweetened chocolate in a microwave-proof bowl. Cover and microwave 1 minute, or until melted. Stir well and set aside. Combine Splenda and water in a small saucepan and bring to a boil. Turn off heat under saucepan. In a medium bowl, beat egg whites and salt on high speed until stiff peaks form. Continue beating on high and pour hot syrup very slowly into beaten egg whites. Set meringue aside.

Beat tofu, melted chocolate, heavy cream, and vanilla until very smooth. Beat in half of meringue. Fold in remaining meringue. Line 8 cupcake pan wells with paper cupcake liners. Spoon approximately $^1/_4$ cup of mousse into each and pack down well. Cover with plastic wrap and freeze about 1 hour. Remove from cupcake pan (you may need to rub the bottom of the pan with a hot, wet washcloth to free the liner) and put into a freezer bag. Store in freezer until ready to serve.

Before serving, let frozen mousse sit at room temperature for 5 minutes before peeling off paper liner.

Makes 8 ($^1/_4$ cup) servings.

● (per serving) Calories 127, Carbohydrates 9 gm, Protein 7 gm, Fat 7 gm, Sat Fat 1 gm, Fiber 1 gm, Cholesterol 5 mg, Sodium 161

Curves Note: For a more traditional mousse, this recipe may be chilled in the refrigerator for at least 2 hours instead of freezing in a cupcake pan.
Curves Tip: To vary the taste of this dessert, use other flavorings instead of vanilla extract, such as 1 teaspoon orange extract or 1 tablespoon creme de menthe liqueur.

(This recipe's ingredients are not included in your shopping list.)

I'M READY FOR THE CURVES DIET
CHECKLIST

_____I have the Curves Weight Loss Method book
Permanent Results without Permanent Dieting

_____I have taken the tests on pages 9 and 10 to
determine which diet plan I should follow

_____I have tried the Curves shake and I know I can drink
it every day

_____I have a blender or shaker to make the Curves shake

_____I have bought the Curves shake

_____I can drink 8 (8-ounce) glasses of water per day

_____I know how to weigh and measure foods

_____I have access to *The Complete Book of Food Counts*
book by Corinne T. Netzer or something like it

_____I know how to look up the calorie and carbohydrate
counts of food

_____I have made sure I have all the foods on the
shopping list on page 72, the foods on the Free
Foods List (page 27), and the pantry essentials on
page 30

_____I have an exercise program that includes strength
training

_____I have gone to Curves to have my beginning weight,
body fat and measurements taken and I have
recorded them in the charts on pages 6 and 7.

SHOPPING LIST–PHASE I

Vegetables

____small can artichoke hearts, canned in water
____*$^1/_2$ cup asparagus
____$^1/_2$ cup broccoli florets
____$^1/_2$ cup carrots, baby
____1 cup cauliflower florets
____3 stalks celery
____*1 cup green beans
____2 green onions
____$^1/_2$ cup green peas
____1 cup mushrooms, sliced
____1 onion
____2 radishes
____2 cups spinach, fresh
____*1 tomato, small
____$^1/_2$ cup zucchini, sliced

_____
_____
_____
_____

Free Foods

____enough for 7 salads

Dairy

____2 tablespoons butter
____2 ounces Cheddar cheese
____2$^1/_2$ cups cottage cheese, lowfat (1%), small curd
____4 eggs
____3 ounces Havarti cheese
____$^1/_2$ gallon milk, skim
____$^1/_2$ ounce Parmesan cheese, grated (2 tablespoons)
____8 ounces yogurt, plain, lowfat

_____
_____

Fruit

____*1 small apple
____$^3/_8$ cup blueberries
____1$^1/_2$ cup cantaloupe, cubed

____*1 grapefruit
____*1 small orange
____$^1/_2$ cup strawberries

_____
_____

Meat and Seafood

____9 breakfast sausage links
____16 ounces chicken breast (divided into 4 portions)
____$^1/_2$ pound ground beef, 93% lean (divided into 2 portions)
____9 ounces ham, lean (divided into 3 portions)
____4-ounce pork chop, lean
____8 ounces orange roughy
____4 ounces roast beef, deli
____4 ounces salmon
____8 ounces shrimp, peeled
____4-ounce sirloin steak, well trimmed
____2 (6-ounce) cans solid white albacore tuna, packed in water
____1 (3-ounce) can solid white albacore tuna, packed in water

_____
_____
_____

Starches

____*2 Keebler Harvest Bakery Multigrain Crackers
____*4 Rye Krisp Crackers
____*4 slices whole wheat bread

_____
_____

Other

____*2 ounces dry roasted peanuts
____*8 ounces V-8 juice

_____

*If you are following the carbohydrate-restricted version, you will not be eating the foods marked with an asterisk, so don't buy them.

PHASE I

Take the tests on pages 9 & 10 to determine whether you are a candidate for the higher protein dieting advantage or whether you should follow the calorie-restricted method.

~

HIGHER PROTEIN/LOW CARBOHYDRATE

For the higher protein/low carbohydrate version, you should:

Enjoy unlimited amounts of lean meats, cheeses, eggs, seafood and poultry (baked, broiled, or boiled—never fried).

Eat moderate to lower amounts of fat.

Limit your carbohydrate intake to 20 grams per day (after subtracting free foods).

Eat, but don't cheat!

If you do not feel that you have adequate energy with this version or if you have not lost weight after a few days, switch to the calorie-restricted method.

CALORIE-RESTRICTED

For the calorie-restricted version, you should:

Eat no more than 1200 calories per day (after subtracting free foods).

Consume 40% of those calories in the form of protein foods.

Consume no more than 60 grams of carbohydrates per day (after subtracting free foods).

~

With either plan you may enjoy one Curves shake per day and unlimited amounts of free foods.

Be sure to drink 8 glasses of water daily and take a good multi-vitamin & mineral supplement.

You will follow Phase I for 1 or 2 weeks. If you have less than 20 pounds to lose you may move to Phase II after 1 week. If you have 20 or more pounds to lose, you will follow Phase I for 2 weeks.

HINT: Circle or highlight free foods in your food diary, so that you can easily subtract them from the totals. See page 39 for an example.

ANOTHER HINT: You are not required to eat the meals in the order they are listed. Feel free to adjust them to your lifestyle and schedule.

PHASE I

EMBRACING CHANGE

List 5 reasons to lose weight:

1. _____
2. _____
3. _____
4. _____
5. _____

List 2 things that will be great about doing this 6-week challenge:

1. _____
   _____
2. _____
   _____

List 4 fears you have about undertaking this challenge :

1. _____
2. _____
3. _____
4. _____

Change is difficult, even change that will have a positive impact on our lives. For any change of habits to have a chance to take root, we must have a plan of action. Jumping into change for emotional reasons is not likely to produce a lasting effect.

In order to get through the pain of dealing with change, you must become comfortable with being uncomfortable. You must believe that the change is for the better, and that it will not always involve the difficulty that it now does. You must be willing to look for bright spots in the midst of what seems like misery.

You can succeed. You have done more difficult things than this, and you have what it takes to follow this plan for six weeks.

GOALS

Setting realistic and measurable goals is one way of keeping your motivation high through this 6-week challenge. Here is an example of a goal that is not helpful:

>a 60 year old woman who is 5 feet tall and weighs 175 pounds wants to look like a super model.

This goal is unrealistic because many super models are only seventeen years old and nearly six feet tall. In addition, this goal is not measurable. A much more helpful set of goals for that fictional woman might be to lose 10-15 pounds of body fat, to work out three times a week, to drink 64 oz. of water every day, and to take a multi-vitamin every day.

Even a seemingly-reasonable goal such as "I want to feel better" is not measurable, and is therefore not a helpful goal. Try to name specific ways you want to feel better (fewer headaches, fewer backaches, fewer upset stomachs, etc.) and attempt to quantify them.

List 8 of your goals:
1. _____
2. _____
3. _____
4. _____
5. _____
6. _____
7. _____
8. _____

Which 2 of your goals are not realistic?
1. _____
2. _____

Which 2 of your goals are not measurable?
1. _____
2. _____

Do you want to set some new goals for yourself? _____
_____
_____
_____

"Do you not know that your body is a temple
of the Holy Spirit, who is in you,
whom you have received from God?

1 Corinthians 6:19

Goals for Monday:

Physical: _____
_____
_____

Mental: _____
_____
_____

Spiritual: _____
_____
_____

What do I hope to change by being on this diet? What are my
goals for this diet? _____
_____
_____
_____
_____

What am I thankful for today? _____
_____
_____

One nice thing I've done for myself today... _____
_____
_____

Be sure to get your beginning weight, body fat and
measurements taken and record them in the charts on
pages 6 and 7.

Day: Monday

		Carbs	Calories
Meal 1	½ cup 1% fat cottage cheese	5	80
	½ cup strawberries	6	23
Meal 2	Curves shake with 8 oz. skim milk	20	200
Meal 3	4 ounces 93% lean ground beef, broiled	0	160
	Free Foods Salad		
Meal 4	⅔ cup tuna salad (recipe page 57)	4	264
	*2 Rye Krisp crackers	11	60
Meal 5	4 ounces chicken breast, broiled	0	124
	Parmesan Vegetable Stir Fry (recipe page 69)	22	275
Meal 6	3 ounces lean ham	0	100
	*1 small apple	20	80

Water: ⬜⬜⬜⬜⬜⬜⬜
Vitamins: ⬭ ⬭ ⬭

	Carbs	Calories
Subtotals		
Minus Free Foods		
Totals for Day		

Today's Exercise:

Curves Workout ♡

or

Aerobic ♡

_____

_____

Strength Training ♡

_____

_____

Stretching ♡

_____

_____

Go to Curves today to be weighed, measured and have your body fat tested. Record your beginning weight, body fat, and measurements on the charts on pages 6 and 7.

If you are following the carbohydrate-restricted version, don't eat the foods that are marked with an asterisk (*). You are allowed to eat unlimited quantities of no-carb foods and free foods.

PHASE I

"I'm just a person trapped inside a woman's body."

—Elayne Boosler

Goals for Tuesday:

Physical: _____

_____

_____

Mental: _____

_____

_____

Spiritual: _____

_____

_____

Do I have certain genetic traits that cannot be changed by improving my eating or exercise habits? (i.e. height, bust size, bone size, shoe size, etc.) _____

_____

_____

_____

_____

_____

_____

_____

_____

What am I thankful for today? _____

_____

_____

One nice thing I've done for myself today... _____

_____

_____

Day: Tuesday

		Carbs	Calories
Meal 1	1 egg	1	75
	*1 sliced tomato	6	30
	*1 slice whole wheat bread	12	70
Meal 2	1/2 cup cubed cantaloupe	6	25
	1/2 cup 1% fat cottage cheese	5	80
Meal 3	4 ounces chicken breast, broiled	0	124
	Free Foods Salad		
Meal 4	Curves shake with 8 oz. skim milk	20	200
Meal 5	4 ounces sirloin steak, broiled	0	215
	1/2 cup steamed broccoli	2	12
	1/2 cup steamed cauliflower	2	13
	1 tablespoon butter	0	102
Meal 6	1 ounce Havarti cheese	0	120
	*1 ounce dry roasted peanuts	5	160

Water: ⊔⊔⊔⊔⊔⊔⊔

Vitamins: ▢ ▢ ▢

	Carbs	Calories
Subtotals		
Minus Free Foods		
Totals for Day		

Today's Exercise:

Curves Workout ♡

or

Aerobic ♡

_____
_____

Strength Training ♡

_____
_____

Stretching ♡

_____
_____

If you are following the carbohydrate-restricted version, don't eat the foods that are marked with an asterisk (*). You are allowed to eat unlimited quantities of no-carb foods and free foods.

"He loves each one of us
as if there were only one of us"
—Augustine

Goals for Wednesday:

Physical: _____

_____

_____

Mental: _____

_____

_____

Spiritual: _____

_____

_____

Do I believe my body is good and worthy of being treated as a creation of God? _____

_____

_____

_____

_____

_____

_____

_____

What am I thankful for today? _____

_____

_____

One nice thing I've done for myself today... _____

_____

_____

80

Day: Wednesday

		Carbs	Calories
Meal 1	4 ounces plain yogurt	9	75
	*¼ cup blueberries	7	27
Meal 2	Curves shake with 8 oz. skim milk	20	200
Meal 3	4 ounces Deli roast beef	4	120
	Free Foods Salad		
Meal 4	⅔ cup tuna salad (recipe page 57)	4	264
	*2 Rye Krisp Crackers	11	60
Meal 5	4 ounces broiled pork chop	0	150
	½ cup zucchini sautéed in:	2	9
	½ tablespoon olive oil	0	60
Meal 6	3 ounces lean ham	0	100
	1 ounce Cheddar cheese	0	110
	Subtotals		
	Minus Free Foods		
	Totals for Day		

Water: 🥛🥛🥛🥛🥛🥛🥛🥛

Vitamins: ⬭ ⬭ ⬭

Today's Exercise:

Curves Workout ♡

or

Aerobic ♡

_____

_____

Strength Training ♡

_____

_____

Stretching ♡

_____

_____

PHASE I

If you are following the carbohydrate-restricted version, don't eat the foods that are marked with an asterisk (*). You are allowed to eat unlimited quantities of no-carb foods and free foods.

"Life itself is the proper binge."

–*Julia Child*

Goals for Thursday:

Physical: _____

_____

_____

Mental: _____

_____

_____

Spiritual: _____

_____

_____

Can I name any eating habits that undermine my ability to eat moderately and healthy? (i.e. binge eating, eating in secret, skipping meals, excessive sugar, salt or fatty-food cravings, etc.) _____

_____

_____

_____

_____

_____

_____

_____

What am I thankful for today? _____

_____

_____

One nice thing I've done for myself today... _____

_____

_____

Day: Thursday

		Carbs	Calories
Meal 1	1 egg	1	75
	3 sausage links	0	200
	*1 piece whole wheat bread	12	70
Meal 2	½ cup 1% fat cottage cheese	5	80
	½ cup baby carrots	5	24
Meal 3	3 ounces water-packed tuna	0	90
	Free Foods Salad		
Meal 4	Curves shake with 8 oz. skim milk	20	200
Meal 5	Stir Fry of:		
	1 tablespoon olive oil	0	120
	4 ounces chicken breast	0	124
	½ cup onions	7	30
	½ cup mushrooms	4	21
	3 artichoke hearts	3	18
	*½ cup asparagus	4	22
Meal 6	1 ounce Havarti cheese	0	120
	*1 medium orange	16	65

Subtotals		
Minus Free Foods		
Totals for Day		

Water: ⬜⬜⬜⬜⬜⬜⬜

Vitamins: ⬭ ⬭ ⬭

Today's Exercise:

Curves Workout ♡

or

Aerobic ♡

_____

_____

Strength Training ♡

_____

_____

Stretching ♡

_____

_____

PHASE I

If you are following the carbohydrate-restricted version, don't eat the foods that are marked with an asterisk (*). You are allowed to eat unlimited quantities of no-carb foods and free foods.

Live in harmony with one another.

PHASE I

Goals for Friday:

Physical: _____

_____

_____

Mental: _____

_____

_____

Spiritual: _____

_____

_____

What areas of my life are out of balance? _____

_____

_____

_____

_____

_____

_____

_____

_____

What am I thankful for today? _____

_____

_____

One nice thing I've done for myself today... _____

_____

_____

_____

_____

Day: Friday

		Carbs	Calories
Meal 1	3 ounces lean ham	0	100
	*1 slice whole wheat bread	12	70
	*1/2 grapefruit	12	46
Meal 2	1/2 cup 1% fat cottage cheese	5	80
	*1/2 cup cubed cantaloupe	6	25
Meal 3	4 ounces broiled salmon	0	207
	1/2 cup green peas	11	60
	1 teaspoon butter	0	34
Meal 4	Curves shake with 8 oz. skim milk	20	200
Meal 5	Free Foods Salad		
Meal 6	2 stalks celery	4	12
	1 ounce Cheddar cheese	0	110
	*1 ounce dry roasted peanuts	5	160

Water: ▯ ▯ ▯ ▯ ▯ ▯ ▯

Vitamins: ⬭ ⬭ ⬭

Subtotals		
Minus Free Foods		
Totals for Day		

Today's Exercise:

Curves Workout ♡

or

Aerobic ♡

_____

_____

Strength Training ♡

_____

_____

Stretching ♡

_____

_____

PHASE I

If you are following the carbohydrate-restricted version, don't eat the foods that are marked with an asterisk (*). You are allowed to eat unlimited quantities of no-carb foods and free foods.

Why are you downcast, O my soul? Why so disturbed within me? Put your hope in God, for I will yet praise him, my Savior and my God.

Psalm 42:5

Goals for Saturday:

Physical: _____

_____

Mental: _____

_____

Spiritual: _____

_____

Do I eat when I'm bored, tired, sad, mad or stressed? _____

_____

_____

_____

_____

_____

_____

What am I thankful for today? _____

_____

_____

One nice thing I've done for myself today... _____

_____

_____

Day: Saturday

		Carbs	Calories
Meal 1	*1 slice whole wheat bread	12	70
	1 ounce Havarti cheese	0	120
	3 sausage links	0	200
Meal 2	Curves shake with 8 oz. skim milk	20	200
Meal 3	Free Foods Salad		
Meal 4	4 ounces 93% hamburger, broiled	0	160
	*8 ounces V-8 juice	10	46
Meal 5	8 ounces shrimp, broiled	0	240
	1⅓ cups French Onion Soup (recipe page 61)	15	199
Meal 6	4 ounces plain yogurt	9	75
	2 tablespoons blueberries	4	14

Water: 🥛🥛🥛🥛🥛🥛🥛🥛

Vitamins: 💊 💊 💊

	Carbs	Calories
Subtotals		
Minus Free Foods		
Totals for Day		

Today's Exercise:

Curves Workout ♡

or

Aerobic ♡

_____

_____

Strength Training ♡

_____

_____

Stretching ♡

_____

_____

PHASE I

If you are following the carbohydrate-restricted version, don't eat the foods that are marked with an asterisk (*). You are allowed to eat unlimited quantities of no-carb foods and free foods.

"Nothing in life is to be feared,
it is only to be understood."

—*Marie Curie*

Goals for Sunday:

Physical: _____

_____

_____

Mental: _____

_____

_____

Spiritual: _____

_____

_____

What do I fear most about being fat? _____

_____

_____

What do I fear most about being thin? _____

_____

_____

What am I thankful for today? _____

_____

_____

One nice thing I've done for myself today... _____

_____

_____

_____

Day: Sunday

		Carbs	Calories
Meal 1	2 eggs	2	150
	3 sausage links	0	200
	*1/2 grapefruit	12	46
Meal 2	4 ounces chicken breast, broiled	0	124
	*1 cup green beans	8	40
Meal 3	Free Foods Salad		
Meal 4	1/2 cup 1% fat cottage cheese	5	80
	1/2 cup cubed cantaloupe	6	25
	*2 Keebler Harvest Bakery Multigrain Crackers	11	70
Meal 5	8 ounces orange roughy sautéed in:	0	216
	1 tablespoon olive oil	0	120
	1 cup spinach	2	12
	1/2 cup steamed cauliflower	3	13
Meal 6	Curves shake with 8 oz. skim milk	20	200

Water: ▯ ▯ ▯ ▯ ▯ ▯ ▯ ▯

Vitamins: ⬭ ⬭ ⬭

	Carbs	Calories
Subtotals		
Minus Free Foods		
Totals for Day		

PHASE I

Today's Exercise:

Curves Workout ♡

or

Aerobic ♡

_____

_____

Strength Training ♡

_____

_____

Stretching ♡

_____

_____

LOOKING AHEAD

Tomorrow you need to go to Curves to be weighed and have your body fat tested. Record your results here:

Weight_____

% Body Fat _____

Pounds of Body Fat _____

Also record your results on the chart on page 7.

If you are following the carbohydrate-restricted version, don't eat the foods that are marked with an asterisk (*). You are allowed to eat unlimited quantities of no-carb foods and free foods.

89

SHOPPING LIST–PHASE II, WEEK 1
(If you have another week on Phase I, use the shopping list on page 72)

Vegetables
____small can artichoke hearts, canned in water
____$1/2$ cup asparagus
____1 cup broccoli florets
____2 stalks celery
____1 cup green beans
____3 green onions
____$1^1/2$ cups mushrooms, sliced
____2 onions
____3 radishes
____$2^1/2$ cups spinach, fresh
____1 tomato, small
____$2^1/2$ cups zucchini, sliced

_____
_____
_____
_____

Free Foods
____enough for 5 salads

Dairy
____1 tablespoon butter
____3 ounces Cheddar cheese
____$1^1/2$ cups cottage cheese, lowfat (1%), small curd
____6 eggs
____4 ounces Havarti cheese
____$1/2$ gallon milk, skim
____1 ounce Parmesan cheese, grated (3 tablespoons)
____4 tablespoons vegetable cream cheese
____20 ounces yogurt, plain, lowfat

_____
_____

Fruit
____1 small apple
____1 banana
____$1/2$ cup blueberries
____1 cup cantaloupe, cubed
____1 small orange
____1 cup strawberries

_____
_____

Meat
____36 ounces chicken breast (divided into 3 (8-ounce) portions and 2 (6-ounce) portions)
____8-ounce pork chop, lean
____6 ounces salmon
____6-ounce sirloin steak, well trimmed
____$1/2$ pound ground beef, 93% lean (divided into 2 portions)
____3 (6-ounce) cans solid white albacore tuna, packed in water
____8 ounces ham, lean
____9 breakfast sausage links
____8 ounces shrimp
____3 ounces extra firm tofu

_____
_____

Starches
____4 Keebler Harvest Bakery Multigrain crackers
____4 Rye Krisp Crackers
____2 slices whole wheat bread

_____
_____

Other
____2 ounces roasted and salted almonds
____$1/2$ cup refried beans
____2 tablespoons salsa
____1 tablespoon Soy sauce
____24 ounces V-8 juice

_____
_____

PHASE I
~ WEEK 2 ~

If you are beginning your second week of Phase I, use the shopping list on page 72. Your food plan is in bold in the following food diaries. You should expect to lose about 2-3 pounds during the second week of Phase I.

~

PHASE II
~ WEEK 1 ~

If you began with less than 20 pounds to lose, you have completed Phase I. You may now move to Phase II, which has a larger amount and variety of food. Use the shopping list on page 90. You should expect to lose 1-2 pounds per week during Phase II. If you are following the higher protein/low carbohydrate method be prepared to switch to the calorie version if:
- *During Phase I, week 1, you lost less than 3 pounds*
- *During Phase I, week 2, you lose less than 2 pounds*
- *During Phase II, any week, you lose less than 1 pound*

~

HIGHER PROTEIN/LOW CARBOHYDRATE

For the higher protein/low carbohydrate version, you should:

Enjoy unlimited amounts of lean meats, cheeses, eggs, seafood and poultry (baked, broiled, or boiled—never fried).

Eat moderate to lower amounts of fat.

Limit your carbohydrate intake to 40-60 grams per day (after subtracting free foods).

Eat, but don't cheat!

CALORIE-RESTRICTED

For the calorie-restricted version, you should:

Eat no more than 1600 calories per day (after subtracting free foods).

Consume 40% of those calories in the form of protein foods.

Consume no more than 60 grams of carbohydrates per day (after subtracting free foods).

~

HINT: Circle or highlight free foods in your food diary, so that you can easily subtract them from the totals. See page 39 for an example.

~
Weekly Lesson #2
~

DIETS DON'T WORK

List 3 dieting methods you have tried:

1. _____
2. _____
3. _____

List 2 dieting methods that have worked for you on a short-term basis:

1. _____
   _____
2. _____
   _____

Name a dieting method that has worked for you and helped you maintain your results for at least 2 years:

_____
_____
_____
_____

Restricting calories causes a decrease in metabolic rate. So why do other diets require us to continue to limit caloric intake?

Don't they know that hormones are produced in response to dieting which allow the body to operate more efficiently? The body is trying to protect us from losing fat, because it doesn't know the difference between intentional dieting and starvation due to famine or disaster. And so, weight loss slows and a plateau is reached on any diet.

When this happens, other diets require us to limit our calories even further. We cannot get ahead of this vicious cycle. Furthermore, so-called maintenance programs are really perpetual diets. Since we now know that perpetual dieting perpetuates a low metabolism, we don't need to feel badly about past failed diets. The problem was not our lack of willpower, the problem was a decreased metabolic rate.

THE CHALLENGE

This 6 week challenge will give you the opportunity to try foods you may have avoided in the past. You may even learn to like some new foods. It will also give you the opportunity to break your addiction to carbohydrates. You should expect to feel remarkably better within the first two weeks. However, you may experience headaches, nausea, and fatigue as your body adjusts to this new way of eating. Don't worry—these symptoms should go away. Drink plenty of water, continue exercising, take your vitamins, and get enough sleep to help yourself through the adjustment period. If you do not feel well on the higher protein/low carbohydrate version, switch to the calorie method.

Some women complain that the daily menu plans contain too much food. Be realistic—you obviously have been eating a lot more food than this on a regular basis, or you wouldn't have a weight problem. Perhaps you are put off by eating more protein. Keep trying and remember that it took time for your body to grow accustomed to the way you used to eat.

Give yourself time to adjust.

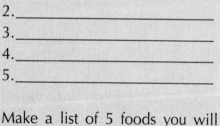

Make a list of the 5 hardest things about this 6 week challenge.

1._____
2._____
3._____
4._____
5._____

Make a list of 5 foods you must give up during this 6 week challenge.

1._____
2._____
3._____
4._____
5._____

Make a list of 5 foods you will enjoy eating during this 6 week challenge.

1._____
2._____
3._____
4._____
5._____

He will yet fill your mouth with laughter
and your lips with shouts of joy.

Job 8:21

Goals for Monday:

Physical: _____
_____
_____

Mental: _____
_____
_____

Spiritual: _____
_____
_____

When was the last time I laughed really hard? _____
_____
_____
_____
_____
_____
_____

What am I thankful for today? _____
_____
_____

One nice thing I've done for myself today... _____
_____
_____
_____
_____

Day: <u>Monday</u>

			Carbs	Calories
Meal 1		½ cup 1% fat cottage cheese	5	80
		½ cup strawberries	6	23
		½ cup 1% fat cottage cheese	**5**	**80**
		½ cup strawberries	**6**	**23**
Meal 2		Curves shake with 8 oz. skim milk	20	200
		Curves shake with 8 oz. skim milk	**20**	**200**
Meal 3		4 ounces 93% lean ground beef, broiled	0	160
		1 cup French Onion Soup (recipe page 61)	15	199
		Free Foods Salad		
		4 ounces 93% lean ground beef, broiled	**0**	**160**
		Free Foods Salad		
Meal 4		⅔ cup tuna salad (recipe page 57)	4	264
		2 Rye Krisp crackers	11	60
		⅔ cup tuna salad (recipe page 57)	**4**	**264**
		***2 Rye Krisp crackers**	**11**	**60**
Meal 5		8 ounces chicken breast, broiled	0	248
		Parmesan Vegetable Stir Fry (recipe page 69)	22	275
		8 ounces V-8 juice	10	46
		4 ounces chicken breast, broiled	**0**	**124**
		Parmesan Vegetable Stir Fry		
		(recipe page 69)	**22**	**275**
Meal 6		2 ounces lean ham	0	67
		1 ounce Havarti cheese	0	120
		3 ounces lean ham	**0**	**100**
		***1 small apple**	**20**	**80**

Water: ☐ ☐ ☐ ☐ ☐ ☐ ☐
Vitamins: ⊖ ⊖ ⊖

Subtotals	
Minus Free Foods	
Totals for Day	

Today's Exercise:

Curves Workout ♡

or

Aerobic ♡

_____

_____

Strength Training ♡

_____

_____

Stretching ♡

_____

_____

PHASE II - 1

If you are doing the 2nd week of Phase I, you need to eat the foods in bold print.

If you are following the carbohydrate-restricted version, (Phase I) don't eat the foods that are marked with an asterisk (*). You are allowed to eat unlimited quantities of no-carb foods and free foods.

"If you follow your bliss...the life that you ought to be living is the one you are living."

—Joseph Campbell

Goals for Tuesday:

Physical: _____
_____
_____

Mental: _____
_____
_____

Spiritual: _____
_____
_____

Do I live in the moment or am I constantly worried about the past or future? _____
_____
_____
_____
_____
_____
_____

What am I thankful for today? _____
_____
_____

One nice thing I've done for myself today... _____
_____
_____
_____

Day: <u>Tuesday</u>

		Carbs	Calories
Meal 1	2 eggs	2	150
	1 sliced tomato	6	30
	1 egg	**1**	**75**
	***1 sliced tomato**	**6**	**30**
	***1 slice whole wheat bread**	**12**	**70**
Meal 2	½ cup cubed cantaloupe	6	25
	½ cup 1% fat cottage cheese	5	80
	1 ounce roasted and salted almonds	4	180
	½ cup cubed cantaloupe	**6**	**25**
	½ cup 1% fat cottage cheese	**5**	**80**
Meal 3	8 ounces chicken breast, broiled	0	248
	Free Foods Salad		
	4 ounces chicken breast, broiled	**0**	**124**
	Free Foods Salad		
Meal 4	Curves shake with 8 oz. skim milk	20	200
	Curves shake with 8 oz. skim milk	**20**	**200**
Meal 5	6 ounces broiled salmon	0	311
	1 cup steamed broccoli	5	24
	1 teaspoon butter	0	34
	4 ounces sirloin steak, broiled	**0**	**215**
	½ cup steamed broccoli	**2**	**12**
	½ cup steamed cauliflower	**2**	**13**
	1 tablespoon butter	**0**	**102**
Meal 6	1 ounce Havarti cheese	0	120
	1 small apple	20	80
	1 ounce Havarti cheese	**0**	**120**
	***1 ounce dry roasted peanuts**	**5**	**160**

Water: 🥛🥛🥛🥛🥛🥛🥛🥛

Vitamins: ⬭ ⬭ ⬭

	Carbs	Calories
Subtotals		
Minus Free Foods		
Totals for Day		

Today's Exercise:

Curves Workout ♡

or

Aerobic ♡

_____

_____

Strength Training ♡

_____

_____

Stretching ♡

_____

_____

If you are doing the 2nd week of Phase I, you need to eat the foods in bold print.

If you are following the carbohydrate-restricted version, (Phase I) don't eat the foods that are marked with an asterisk (*). You are allowed to eat unlimited quantities of no-carb foods and free foods.

For I am the Lord, your God,
who takes hold of your right hand and says to you:
Do not fear; I will help you.

Isaiah 41:13

Goals for Wednesday:

Physical: _____
_____
_____

Mental: _____
_____
_____

Spiritual: _____
_____
_____

Is there any significant person in my life who does not
support my efforts to change? _____
_____
_____
_____
_____
_____

What am I thankful for today? _____
_____
_____

One nice thing I've done for myself today... _____
_____
_____
_____

Day: Wednesday

		Carbs	Calories
Meal 1	8 ounces plain yogurt	18	150
	1/4 cup blueberries	7	27
	4 ounces plain yogurt	**9**	**75**
	***1/4 cup blueberries**	**7**	**27**
Meal 2	Curves shake with 8 oz. skim milk	20	200
	Curves shake with 8 oz. skim milk	**20**	**200**
Meal 3	1 serving Spinach Salad (page 58)		
	with 2 tablespoons Orange Vinaigrette	11	138
	8 ounces chicken breast, broiled	0	248
	4 ounces Deli roast beef	**4**	**120**
	Free Foods Salad		
Meal 4	2/3 cup tuna salad (recipe page 57)	4	264
	2 Rye Krisp Crackers	11	60
	8 ounces V-8 juice	10	46
	2/3 cup tuna salad (recipe page 57)	**4**	**264**
	***2 Rye Krisp Crackers**	**11**	**60**
Meal 5	6 ounces broiled sirloin steak	0	323
	1 cup zucchini sautéed in:	4	18
	1 tablespoon olive oil	0	120
	4 ounces broiled pork chop	**0**	**150**
	1/2 cup zucchini sautéed in:	**2**	**9**
	1/2 tablespoon olive oil	**0**	**60**
Meal 6	3 ounces lean ham	0	100
	1 ounce Havarti cheese	0	120
	3 ounces lean ham	**0**	**100**
	1 ounce Cheddar cheese	**0**	**110**

Water: ⊔ ⊔ ⊔ ⊔ ⊔ ⊔ ⊔
Vitamins: ⊂⊃ ⊂⊃ ⊂⊃

	Carbs	Calories
Subtotals		
Minus Free Foods		
Totals for Day		

Today's Exercise:

Curves Workout ♡

or

Aerobic ♡

_____

_____

Strength Training ♡

_____

_____

Stretching ♡

_____

_____

PHASE II - 1

If you are doing the 2nd week of Phase I, you need to eat the foods in bold print.

If you are following the carbohydrate-restricted version, (Phase I) don't eat the foods that are marked with an asterisk (*). You are allowed to eat unlimited quantities of no-carb foods and free foods.

*"To love and be loved is to
feel the sun from both sides."*

—David Viscott

Goals for Thursday:

Physical: _____

_____

_____

Mental: _____

_____

_____

Spiritual: _____

_____

_____

Do I like myself? Do I love myself? _____

_____

_____

_____

_____

_____

_____

_____

What am I thankful for today? _____

_____

_____

One nice thing I've done for myself today... _____

_____

_____

_____

_____

Day: <u>Thursday</u>

		Carbs	Calories
Meal 1	2 eggs	2	150
	3 sausage links	0	200
	1 piece whole wheat bread	12	70
	1 egg	**1**	**75**
	3 sausage links	**0**	**200**
	*1 piece whole wheat bread	**12**	**70**
Meal 2	2 Keebler Harvest Bakery Multigrain crackers	11	70
	2 tablespoons vegetable cream cheese	2	90
	$^1/_2$ cup 1% fat cottage cheese	**5**	**80**
	$^1/_2$ cup baby carrots	**5**	**24**
Meal 3	Stir Fry of:		
	1 tablespoon olive oil	0	120
	6 ounces chicken breast	0	186
	$^1/_2$ cup onions	7	30
	$^1/_2$ cup mushrooms	4	21
	3 artichoke hearts	3	18
	$^1/_2$ cup asparagus	4	22
	Curves shake with 8 oz. skim milk	**20**	**200**
Meal 4	Curves shake with 8 oz. skim milk	20	200
	3 ounces water-packed tuna	**0**	**90**
	Free Foods Salad		
Meal 5	Beef Tenderloin with Blue Cheese (recipe page 63)	1	383
	Free Foods Salad		
	Stir Fry of: 1 tablespoon olive oil	**0**	**120**
	4 ounces chicken breast	**0**	**124**
	$^1/_2$ cup onions	**7**	**30**
	$^1/_2$ cup mushrooms	**4**	**21**
	3 artichoke hearts	**3**	**18**
	*$^1/_2$ cup asparagus	**4**	**22**
Meal 6	$^1/_2$ banana	13	53
	1 ounce cheddar cheese	0	110
	1 ounce Havarti cheese	**0**	**120**
	*1 medium orange	**16**	**65**

	Carbs	Calories
Subtotals		
Minus Free Foods		
Totals for Day		

Water: ⊔ ⊔ ⊔ ⊔ ⊔ ⊔ ⊔

Vitamins: ⊂⊃ ⊂⊃ ⊂⊃

Today's Exercise:

Curves Workout ♡

or

Aerobic ♡

_____

_____

Strength Training ♡

_____

_____

Stretching ♡

_____

_____

If you are doing the 2nd week of Phase I, you need to eat the foods in bold print.

If you are following the carbohydrate-restricted version, (Phase I) don't eat the foods that are marked with an asterisk (*). You are allowed to eat unlimited quantities of no-carb foods and free foods.

"You need the serenity to accept the things you cannot change, the courage to change the things you can and the wisdom to know the difference."

—Reinhold Niebuhr

Goals for Friday:

Physical: _____

_____

Mental: _____

_____

Spiritual: _____

_____

How do I feel about changes in my life? _____

_____

_____

_____

_____

_____

What am I thankful for today? _____

_____

_____

One nice thing I've done for myself today... _____

_____

_____

_____

_____

Day: Friday

		Carbs	Calories
Meal 1	8 ounces plain yogurt	18	150
	1/2 cup strawberries	6	23
	3 ounces lean ham	**0**	**100**
	***1 slice whole wheat bread**	**12**	**70**
	***1/2 grapefruit**	**12**	**46**
Meal 2	Curves shake with 8 oz. skim milk	20	200
	1/2 cup 1% fat cottage cheese	**5**	**80**
	***1/2 cup cubed cantaloupe**	**6**	**25**
Meal 3	8 ounces pork chop, lean, broiled	0	300
	1 cup zucchini, sautéed in:	4	18
	1 tablespoon olive oil	0	120
	Free Foods Salad		
	4 ounces broiled salmon	**0**	**207**
	1/2 cup green peas	**11**	**60**
	1 teaspoon butter	**0**	**34**
Meal 4	1 ounce Cheddar cheese	0	110
	3 ounces lean ham	0	100
	Curves shake with 8 oz. skim milk	**20**	**200**
Meal 5	2 Keebler Harvest Bakery Multigrain crackers	11	70
	2 tablespoons vegetable cream cheese	2	90
	Free Foods Salad		
Meal 6	2/3 cup tuna salad (recipe page 57)	4	264
	2 stalks celery	**4**	**12**
	1 ounce Cheddar cheese	**0**	**110**
	***1 ounce dry roasted peanuts**	**5**	**160**

Water: 🥛🥛🥛🥛🥛🥛🥛

Vitamins: ⬭ ⬭ ⬭

Subtotals	
Minus Free Foods	
Totals for Day	

Curves Workout ♡

or

Aerobic ♡
_____
_____

Strength Training ♡
_____
_____

Stretching ♡
_____
_____

PHASE II - 1

If you are doing the 2nd week of Phase I, you need to eat the foods in bold print.

If you are following the carbohydrate-restricted version, (Phase I) don't eat the foods that are marked with an asterisk (*). You are allowed to eat unlimited quantities of no-carb foods and free foods.

And do not set your heart on what you
will eat or drink; do not worry about it.

Goals for Saturday:

Physical: _____
_____
_____

Mental: _____
_____
_____

Spiritual: _____
_____
_____

Do I live to eat or eat to live? _____
_____
_____
_____
_____
_____
_____
_____

What am I thankful for today? _____
_____
_____

One nice thing I've done for myself today... _____
_____
_____
_____
_____

Day: Saturday

		Carbs	Calories
Meal 1	1 slice whole wheat bread	12	70
	1 ounce Havarti cheese	0	120
	3 sausage links	0	200
	*1 slice whole wheat bread	**12**	**70**
	1 ounce Havarti cheese	**0**	**120**
	3 sausage links	**0**	**200**
Meal 2	Curves shake with 8 oz. skim milk	20	200
	Curves shake with 8 oz. skim milk	**20**	**200**
Meal 3	4 ounces 93% lean ground beef, broiled	0	160
	1 ounce Cheddar cheese	0	110
	1/2 cup refried beans	25	120
	2 tablespoons salsa	2	10
	Free Foods Salad		
Meal 4	1 ounce roasted and salted almonds	4	180
	4 ounces 93% hamburger, broiled	**0**	**160**
	*8 ounces V-8 juice	**10**	**46**
Meal 5	Tofu Stir Fry (recipe page 68)	25	440
	8 ounces shrimp, broiled	**0**	**240**
	1 1/3 cups French Onion Soup		
	(recipe page 61)	**15**	**199**
Meal 6	4 ounces plain yogurt	9	75
	2 tablespoons blueberries	4	14
	4 ounces plain yogurt	**9**	**75**
	2 tablespoons blueberries	**4**	**14**

Water: ▯ ▯ ▯ ▯ ▯ ▯ ▯ ▯

Vitamins: ⬭ ⬭ ⬭

	Carbs	Calories
Subtotals		
Minus Free Foods		
Totals for Day		

Today's Exercise:

Curves Workout ♡

or

Aerobic ♡

_____

_____

Strength Training ♡

_____

_____

Stretching ♡

_____

_____

PHASE II - 1

If you are doing the 2nd week of Phase I, you need to eat the foods in bold print.

If you are following the carbohydrate-restricted version, (Phase I) don't eat the foods that are marked with an asterisk (*). You are allowed to eat unlimited quantities of no-carb foods and free foods.

"Come to me, all you who are weary
and burdened, and I will give you rest.

Matthew 11:28

Goals for Sunday:

Physical: _____

_____

_____

Mental: _____

_____

_____

Spiritual: _____

_____

_____

Do I feel like I get enough sleep at night? How many hours do I sleep on average? _____

_____

_____

_____

_____

_____

_____

What am I thankful for today? _____

_____

_____

One nice thing I've done for myself today... _____

_____

_____

_____

_____

Day: Sunday

		Carbs	Calories
Meal 1	2 eggs	2	150
	3 sausage links	0	200
	8 ounces V-8 juice	10	46
	2 eggs	**2**	**150**
	3 sausage links	**0**	**200**
	*1/2 grapefruit	**12**	**46**
Meal 2	1/2 cup 1% fat cottage cheese	5	80
	1/2 cup cubed cantaloupe	6	25
	4 ounces chicken breast, broiled	**0**	**124**
	*1 cup green beans	**8**	**40**
Meal 3	6 ounces chicken breast, broiled	0	186
	1 cup green beans	8	40
	1 tablespoon Parmesan cheese	0	28
	Free Foods Salad		
	Free Foods Salad		
Meal 4	1 serving Spicy Zucchini Boats (2 pieces) (recipe page 54)	5	210
	Curves shake with 8 oz. skim milk	**20**	**200**
Meal 5	8 ounces shrimp, sautéed in:	0	240
	1 tablespoon olive oil	0	120
	1 cup spinach	2	12
	1 medium orange	16	65
	8 ounces orange roughy sautéed in:	**0**	**216**
	1 tablespoon olive oil	**0**	**120**
	1 cup spinach	**2**	**12**
	1/2 cup steamed cauliflower	**3**	**13**
Meal 6	Curves shake with 8 oz. skim milk	20	200
	1/2 cup 1% fat cottage cheese	**5**	**80**
	1/2 cup cubed cantaloupe	**6**	**25**
	*2 Keebler Harvest Bakery Multigrain Crackers	**11**	**70**

Water: 🥛🥛🥛🥛🥛🥛🥛

Vitamins: 💊💊💊

Subtotals		
Minus Free Foods		
Totals for Day		

Today's Exercise:

Curves Workout ♡

or

Aerobic ♡

_____

_____

Strength Training ♡

_____

_____

Stretching ♡

_____

_____

LOOKING AHEAD

Tomorrow you need to go to Curves to be weighed and have your body fat tested. Record your results here:

Weight_____

% Body Fat _____

Pounds of Body Fat _____

Also record your results on the chart on page 7.

If you are doing the 2nd week of Phase I, you need to eat the foods in bold print.

SHOPPING LIST–PHASE II, WEEK 2

Vegetables
____$1/2$ cup asparagus
____1 cup carrots
____1 cup cauliflower florets
____2 stalks celery
____1 cup green beans
____3 green onions
____$1/2$ cup green peas
____$1^1/2$ cups mushrooms, sliced
____2 onions
____3 radishes
____$2^1/2$ cups spinach, fresh
____$1^1/2$ cups zucchini, sliced

_____
_____
_____

Free Foods
____enough for 5 salads

Dairy
____2 tablespoons butter
____3 ounces Cheddar cheese
____$1^1/2$ cups cottage cheese, lowfat (1%), small curd
____5 eggs
____5 ounces Havarti cheese
____$1/2$ gallon milk, skim
____1 ounce Parmesan cheese, grated (3 tablespoons)
____2 tablespoons vegetable cream cheese
____8 ounces yogurt, plain, lowfat

_____
_____

Fruit
____1 small apple
____$1/4$ cup blueberries
____1 cup cantaloupe, cubed
____1 small orange
____1 cup strawberries
____$1/2$ cup watermelon, cubed

_____
_____

Meat
____28 ounces chicken breast (divided into 2 (8-ounce) portions and 2 (6-ounce) portions)
____10 ounces ground beef, 93% lean (divided)
____12 ounces ham, lean
____8 ounces orange roughy
____9 breakfast sausage links
____6 ounces light smoked sausage
____8 ounces shrimp
____3 ounces extra firm tofu
____3 (6-ounce) cans solid white albacore tuna, packed in water

_____
_____
_____
_____

Starches
____4 Keebler Harvest Bakery Multigrain crackers
____2 pieces Holland Rusk Dry Toast
____4 Rye Krisp crackers
____1 slice whole wheat bread

_____
_____

Other
____3 ounces roasted and salted cashews
____$1/2$ cup refried beans
____4 ounces rosé wine
____$1/2$ cup sauerkraut
____2 tablespoons salsa
____1 tablespoon Soy sauce
____24 ounces V-8 juice

_____
_____
_____

PHASE II

~ WEEK 2 ~

You should expect to lose 1-2 pounds per week during Phase II.
Your weight loss will begin to slow as your metabolism decreases. Losing a pound or
more of body fat weekly is worth the effort.
If you are following the higher protein method and your weight loss drops below
1 pound per week during Phase II,
you should switch to the calorie-restricted version.

~

HIGHER PROTEIN/LOW CARBOHYDRATE

For the higher protein/low carbohydrate version, you should:

Enjoy unlimited amounts of lean meats, cheeses, eggs, seafood and poultry
(baked, broiled, or boiled—never fried).

Eat moderate to lower amounts of fat.
Limit your carbohydrate intake to 40-60 grams per day
(after subtracting free foods).

Eat, but don't cheat!

CALORIE-RESTRICTED

For the calorie-restricted version, you should:

Eat no more than 1600 calories per day
(after subtracting free foods).

Consume 40% of those calories in the form of protein foods.

Consume no more than 60 grams of carbohydrates per day
(after subtracting free foods).

~

HINT: Circle or highlight free foods in your food diary, so that you can
easily subtract them from the totals. See page 39 for an example.

ANOTHER HINT: You are not required to eat the meals in the order they
are listed. Feel free to adjust them to your lifestyle and schedule.

PHASE II - 2

EXERCISE HELPS

Strength training protects muscle mass, even while we are losing weight. Women sometimes avoid strength training because they do not want to develop huge muscles. The strength training component of the Curves Workout will not encourage development of bulky muscles.

Aerobic exercise (cardio) is a vital part of our fitness plan. It conditions your body to better utilize body fat. If your goal is to attain a moderate level of fitness and encourage weight loss, you do not need to raise your heart rate above 60% to 70% of its maximum capacity.

Another part of our plan is stretching, which helps prevent soreness after a workout and can also help to prevent injuries. Always stretch after your workout.

Along with warming up and cooling down, strength training, cardio, and stretching make up a complete workout.

List the five components of a balanced workout:

1. _____
2. _____
3. _____
4. _____
5. _____

What are your three favorite types of exercise?

1. _____
   _____
2. _____
   _____
3. _____
   _____

Why do you like them?

_____
_____
_____
_____

PHASE II - 2

DON'T QUIT

It is too easy to confuse disappointment with disaster. Maybe you haven't done a very good job of sticking to the 6 week challenge plan so far. Maybe you have only made it to Curves one time and haven't done any other form of exercise. Maybe you fell off the wagon just last week by going out to dinner and eating lots of bread and pasta. Every day is a new day and every meal is a chance to regain your good habits. Don't let your lack of perfection give you an excuse to quit.

Maybe other people are getting more results than you are. Don't let it get you down. You can only be responsible for your own body. Choose to be inspired by the good things happening to others—don't be jealous or mad.

All any of us can do is the best we can do, every day. So choose to do your best and don't give up. Remember that two steps forward and one step back will still get you there.

List 3 reasons you have been tempted to quit this 6-week challenge:
1._____
2._____
3._____

List 3 reasons to stick with it:
1._____
2._____
3._____

Describe your worst failure in following the plan so far:

_____
_____
_____
_____

Bear with each other and forgive whatever grievances you may have against one another. Forgive as the Lord forgave you.

Colossians 3:13

Goals for Monday:

Physical: _____

_____

_____

Mental: _____

_____

_____

Spiritual: _____

_____

_____

Is there any relationship in my life that needs forgiveness and healing? _____

_____

_____

_____

_____

_____

What am I thankful for today? _____

_____

_____

One nice thing I've done for myself today... _____

_____

_____

Day: Monday

		Carbs	Calories
Meal 1	1/2 cup 1% fat cottage cheese	5	80
	1/2 cup strawberries	6	23
Meal 2	Curves shake with 8 oz. skim milk	20	200
Meal 3	4 ounces 93% lean ground beef, broiled	0	160
	1 cup cooked carrots	11	48
	1 teaspoon butter	0	34
	Free Foods Salad		
Meal 4	2/3 cup tuna salad (recipe page 57)	4	264
	2 Rye Krisp crackers	11	60
Meal 5	8 ounces chicken breast, broiled	0	248
	Parmesan Vegetable Stir Fry (recipe page 69)	22	275
	8 ounces V-8 juice	10	46
Meal 6	3 ounces lean ham	0	100
	1 ounce Havarti cheese	0	120

Water: ⬜⬜⬜⬜⬜⬜⬜⬜

Vitamins: ⬭⬭⬭

	Carbs	Calories
Subtotals		
Minus Free Foods		
Totals for Day		

Today's Exercise:

Curves Workout ♡

or

Aerobic ♡

_____

_____

Strength Training ♡

_____

_____

Stretching ♡

_____

_____

TIP:
The ingredients for most recipes are not included in your shopping list—plan ahead so you are prepared.

"Everyone wants to live on top of the mountain, but all the happiness and growth occurs from climbing it."

—Author unknown

Goals for Tuesday:

Physical: _____

_____

_____

Mental: _____

_____

_____

Spiritual: _____

_____

_____

When was the last time I had fun with others? _____

_____

_____

_____

_____

_____

_____

_____

What am I thankful for today? _____

_____

_____

One nice thing I've done for myself today... _____

_____

_____

_____

_____

Day: Tuesday

		Carbs	Calories
Meal 1	2 eggs	2	150
	3 ounces ham, lean	0	100
	1 piece Holland Rusk Dry Toast	6	30
Meal 2	1/2 cup cubed cantaloupe	6	25
	1/2 cup 1% fat cottage cheese	5	80
	1 ounce roasted and salted cashews	7	170
Meal 3	Greek Salad (recipe page 59)	14	383
Meal 4	Curves shake with 8 oz. skim milk	20	200
Meal 5	8 ounces broiled orange roughy	0	216
	1 cup steamed cauliflower	5	26
	1 tablespoon butter	0	102
	1 cup French Onion Soup (recipe page 61)	15	199
Meal 6	1 ounce Havarti cheese	0	120
	1 small apple	20	80

Today's Exercise:

Curves Workout ♡

or

Aerobic ♡

_____

_____

Strength Training ♡

_____

_____

Stretching ♡

_____

_____

Water: ⊔ ⊔ ⊔ ⊔ ⊔ ⊔ ⊔

Vitamins: ⊂⊃ ⊂⊃ ⊂⊃

	Carbs	Calories
Subtotals		
Minus Free Foods		
Totals for Day		

"I thought in my heart, 'Come now, I will test you
with pleasure to find out what is good.'
But that also proved to be meaningless."

Ecclesiastes 2:1

Goals for Wednesday:

Physical: _____
_____
_____

Mental: _____
_____

Spiritual: _____
_____
_____

What bores me? _____
_____
_____
_____
_____
_____

What am I thankful for today? _____
_____
_____

One nice thing I've done for myself today... _____
_____
_____
_____

Day: Wednesday

		Carbs	Calories
Meal 1	4 ounces plain yogurt	9	75
	1/4 cup blueberries	7	27
Meal 2	Curves shake with 8 oz. skim milk	20	200
Meal 3	1 serving Spinach Salad (recipe page 58)		
	with 2 tablespoons Orange Vinaigrette	11	138
	8 ounces chicken breast, broiled	0	248
Meal 4	2/3 cup tuna salad (recipe page 57)	4	264
	2 Rye Krisp Crackers	11	60
	8 ounces V-8 juice	10	46
Meal 5	6 ounces light smoked sausage	12	330
	1/2 cup sauerkraut	5	20
	1 cup zucchini sautéed in:	4	18
	1 tablespoon olive oil	0	120
Meal 6	3 ounces lean ham	0	100
	1 ounce Havarti cheese	0	120

Water: 🥛🥛🥛🥛🥛🥛🥛
Vitamins: ⬭ ⬭ ⬭

	Carbs	Calories
Subtotals		
Minus Free Foods		
Totals for Day		

Today's Exercise:

Curves Workout ♡

or

Aerobic ♡

_____

_____

Strength Training ♡

_____

_____

Stretching ♡

_____

_____

TIP:
Plain lowfat yogurt and 1% cottage cheese are interchangeable in equal amounts.

"Twenty years from now you will be more disappointed by the things that you didn't do than by the ones you did do. So throw off the bowlines. Sail away from the safe harbor. Catch the trade winds in your sails. Explore. Dream. Discover."

—Mark Twain

Goals for Thursday:

Physical: _____

_____

_____

Mental: _____

_____

_____

Spiritual: _____

_____

_____

What never bores me? _____

_____

_____

_____

_____

_____

_____

What am I thankful for today? _____

_____

_____

One nice thing I've done for myself today... _____

_____

_____

Day: Thursday

		Carbs	Calories
Meal 1	2 eggs	2	150
	3 sausage links	0	200
	1 piece Holland Rusk Dry Toast	6	30
Meal 2	2 Keebler Harvest Bakery Multigrain crackers	11	70
	2 tablespoons vegetable cream cheese	2	90
Meal 3	Sherry-Mushroom Chicken (recipe page 66)	8	314
	1/2 cup steamed asparagus	4	22
	1 teaspoon butter	0	34
	Free Foods Salad		
Meal 4	Curves shake with 8 oz. skim milk	20	200
Meal 5	Stir Fry of:		
	1 tablespoon olive oil	0	120
	6 ounces chicken breast	0	186
	1/2 cup onions	7	30
	1/2 cup mushrooms	4	21
	1/2 cup green peas	11	60
Meal 6	1 ounce roasted and salted cashews	7	170
	1/2 cup cubed watermelon	6	25
	1 ounce cheddar cheese	0	110

Water: ☐ ☐ ☐ ☐ ☐ ☐ ☐

Vitamins: ☐ ☐ ☐

	Carbs	Calories
Subtotals		
Minus Free Foods		
Totals for Day		

Today's Exercise:

Curves Workout ♡

or

Aerobic ♡

_____

_____

Strength Training ♡

_____

_____

Stretching ♡

_____

_____

PHASE II - 2

119

"Habit is either the best of servants
or the worst of masters."

– Nathaniel Emmons

Goals for Friday:

Physical: _____

_____

_____

Mental: _____

_____

_____

Spiritual: _____

_____

_____

How important is food to you? Do you think of it very often?
Do you feel disciplined in your management of food?

_____

_____

_____

_____

_____

_____

_____

_____

What am I thankful for today? _____

_____

_____

One nice thing I've done for myself today... _____

_____

_____

Day: Friday

		Carbs	Calories
Meal 1	4 ounces plain yogurt	9	75
	1/2 cup strawberries	6	23
Meal 2	Curves shake with 8 oz. skim milk	20	200
Meal 3	1 serving Easy Frittata (recipe page 64)	16	384
	Free Foods Salad		
Meal 4	3 ounces lean ham	0	100
	1 orange	16	65
Meal 5	2 Keebler Harvest Bakery Multigrain crackers	11	70
	1 ounce Cheddar cheese	0	110
Meal 6	2/3 cup tuna salad (recipe page 57)	4	264

Water: ☐ ☐ ☐ ☐ ☐ ☐ ☐
Vitamins: ☐ ☐ ☐

Subtotals		
Minus Free Foods		
Totals for Day		

Today's Exercise:

Curves Workout ♡

or

Aerobic ♡

_____

_____

Strength Training ♡

_____

_____

Stretching ♡

_____

_____

PHASE II - 2

TIP:
Don't forget to stretch after your workout — your body will thank you!

121

Therefore do not worry about tomorrow,
for tomorrow will worry about itself.
Each day has enough trouble of its own.

Matthew 6:34

Goals for Saturday:

Physical: _____

_____

_____

Mental: _____

_____

_____

Spiritual: _____

_____

_____

What am I worried or concerned about today? _____

_____

_____

_____

_____

_____

_____

What am I thankful for today? _____

_____

_____

One nice thing I've done for myself today... _____

_____

_____

_____

_____

Day: Saturday

		Carbs	Calories
Meal 1	1 slice whole wheat bread	12	70
	1 ounce Havarti cheese	0	120
	3 sausage links	0	200
Meal 2	Curves shake with 8 oz. skim milk	20	200
Meal 3	6 ounces 93% lean ground beef, broiled	0	240
	1 ounce Cheddar cheese	0	110
	1/2 cup refried beans	25	120
	2 tablespoons salsa	2	10
Meal 4	1 ounce roasted and salted cashews	7	170
	4 ounces V-8 juice	5	23
Meal 5	Free Foods Salad		
Meal 6	Tofu Stir Fry (recipe page 68)	25	440

Today's Exercise:

Curves Workout ♡

or

Aerobic ♡

_____

_____

Strength Training ♡

_____

_____

Stretching ♡

_____

_____

Water: 🥛🥛🥛🥛🥛🥛🥛

Vitamins: ⬭ ⬭ ⬭

	Carbs	Calories
Subtotals		
Minus Free Foods		
Totals for Day		

PHASE II - 2

123

"The Hunger for Love is much more difficult
to remove than the Hunger for Bread"
— *Mother Teresa*

Goals for Sunday:

Physical: _____

_____

_____

Mental: _____

_____

_____

Spiritual: _____

_____

_____

Am I trying to fill a void in my life by eating? by exercising? by dieting? _____

_____

_____

_____

_____

What am I thankful for today? _____

_____

_____

One nice thing I've done for myself today... _____

_____

_____

_____

Reminder - Go to Curves tomorrow to be measured and have your weight and body fat tested. Record your results in the charts on page 6 and 7.

Day: Sunday

		Carbs	Calories
Meal 1	1 egg	1	75
	3 sausage links	0	200
	4 ounces V-8 juice	5	25
Meal 2	½ cup 1% fat cottage cheese	5	80
	½ cup cubed cantaloupe	6	25
Meal 3	6 ounces chicken breast, broiled	0	186
	1 cup green beans	8	40
	1 tablespoon Parmesan cheese	0	28
	Free Foods Salad		
Meal 4	1 ounce Havarti cheese	0	120
	4 ounce glass of rosé wine	6	100
Meal 5	8 ounces shrimp sautéed in:	0	240
	1 tablespoon olive oil	0	120
	1 cup spinach	2	12
	1 orange	16	65
Meal 6	Curves shake with 8 oz. skim milk	20	200

Water: 🥛🥛🥛🥛🥛🥛

Vitamins: ⬭⬭⬭

	Carbs	Calories
Subtotals		
Minus Free Foods		
Totals for Day		

Today's Exercise:

Curves Workout ♡

or

Aerobic ♡

_____

_____

Strength Training ♡

_____

_____

Stretching ♡

_____

_____

Tomorrow you need to go to Curves to be weighed and have your body fat tested. Record your results here:

Weight_____

% Body Fat _____

Pounds of
Body Fat _____

Record your results on the chart on page 7. You also need to have measurements taken and recorded in the chart on page 6 (Week 4 Measurements)

PHASE II - 2

SHOPPING LIST–PHASE II, WEEK 3

Vegetables

____¹/₂ cup asparagus
____1 cup broccoli florets
____1 cup carrots
____1 stalk celery
____1 cup green beans
____2 green onions
____¹/₂ cup mushrooms, sliced
____1 onion
____2 radishes
____¹/₂ cup snow peas
____2 cups spinach, fresh
____1 cup zucchini, sliced

_____
_____
_____

Free Foods

____enough for 6 salads

Dairy

____3 tablespoons butter
____3 ounces Cheddar cheese
____2 cups cottage cheese,
    lowfat (1%), small curd
____7 eggs
____5 ounces Havarti cheese
____¹/₂ gallon milk, skim
____¹/₂ ounce Parmesan cheese,
    grated (2 tablespoons)
____2 tablespoons vegetable
    cream cheese
____8 ounces yogurt, plain,
    lowfat

_____
_____
_____

Fruit

____1 small apple
____¹/₄ cup blueberries
____1¹/₂ cup cantaloupe, cubed
____1 small orange
____¹/₂ cup strawberries
____¹/₂ cup watermelon, cubed

_____

_____
_____
_____

Meat and Seafood

____14 ounces chicken breast
    (divided into 1 (8 ounce) and
    1 (6 ounce) portions
____6-ounce pork chop, lean
____4 ounces salmon
____¹/₂ pound ground beef,
    93% lean (divided)
____2 (6-ounce) cans solid white
    albacore tuna, packed in
    water
____12 ounces ham, lean
____9 breakfast sausage links
____8 ounces shrimp
____8 ounces orange roughy
____6 ounces light smoked
    sausage

_____
_____
_____

Starches

____2 pieces Holland Rusk
    Dry Toast
____2 Keebler Harvest Bakery
    Multigrain crackers
____4 Rye Krisp crackers
____2 slices whole wheat bread

_____

Other

____1 tablespoon barbeque sauce
____3 ounces roasted and salted
    cashews
____¹/₂ cup refried beans
____2 tablespoons salsa
____¹/₂ cup sauerkraut
____12 ounces V-8 juice
____4 ounces rosé wine

_____
_____

PHASE II - 2

PHASE II

~ WEEK 3 ~

*As long as you are losing at least 1 pound per week you should continue on Phase II.
If your weight loss drops below 1 pound per week during Phase II,
even after switching to the calorie-restricted version,
you should move to Phase III because you have hit a plateau.*

~

HIGHER PROTEIN/LOW CARBOHYDRATE

For the higher protein/low carbohydrate version, you should:

Enjoy unlimited amounts of lean meats, cheeses, eggs, seafood and poultry
(baked, broiled, or boiled—never fried).

Eat moderate to lower amounts of fat.
Limit your carbohydrate intake to 40-60 grams per day
(after subtracting free foods).

Eat, but don't cheat!

CALORIE-RESTRICTED

For the calorie-restricted version, you should:

Eat no more than 1600 calories per day
(after subtracting free foods).

Consume 40% of those calories in the form of protein foods.

Consume no more than 60 grams of carbohydrates per day
(after subtracting free foods).

~

PHASE II - 3

HINT: Circle or highlight free foods in your food diary, so that you can
easily subtract them from the totals. See page 39 for an example.

ANOTHER HINT: You are not required to eat the meals in the order they
are listed. Feel free to adjust them to your lifestyle and schedule.

127

SELF LABELS & SELF TALK

List 6 of your good qualities:
1. _____
2. _____
3. _____
4. _____
5. _____
6. _____

List 3 nice names for yourself:
1. _____
2. _____
3. _____

Write a daily affirmation for yourself:
_____
_____
_____
_____
_____
_____

Children get stuck with labels and nicknames that may or may not have any basis in truth. Perhaps your childhood nickname was "trouble." Are you still "trouble?" Maybe you were "Mommy's good girl." Does that feel like a burden now?

As adults, we are free to create our own self labels. It is good to work on thinking of yourself in complimentary terms. People who care about you are already referring to you by nice names.

Self talk is going on in your head all day long. So take the opportunity to say nice things to yourself. Congratulate yourself for doing your best on this 6-week challenge. Praise yourself for learning to enjoy different foods. Acknowledge your right to put your needs ahead of the needs of others for a while.

PHASE II - 3

HABITS

It takes about 30 days to acquire a habit—good or bad. At this point in the 6 week challenge, you should be acquiring some new habits. The day to day part of following the plan should be getting easier, because it should be becoming routine. If you are trying to drop a lot of bad habits during this 6 week challenge, you may be struggling. Keep doing the best you can every day. Now is not the time to give up. You have just three more weeks to complete the challenge.

Perhaps some of your customs are getting in the way of following the plan. For instance, if you are a late night snacker, maybe you could go to bed sooner. If you like to eat popcorn with your family while you watch TV, could you eat celery or a small amount of nuts instead? Could you watch less TV? Could you keep your hands busy with needlework or knitting?

Try to make your habits work to your advantage.

List 3 habits that are making it difficult for you to follow the plan:
1._____
2._____
3._____

List 3 things you can do to circumvent those habits:
1._____
2._____
3._____

List 3 good new habits you have gained so far:
1._____
2._____
3._____

Do not judge, and you will not be judged.
Do not condemn, and you will not be condemned.
Forgive, and you will be forgiven.

Luke 6:37

Goals for Monday:

Physical: _____

_____

Mental: _____

_____

Spiritual: _____

_____

Is there anyone I am unwilling to forgive? Is there anyone I do not want to talk to? _____

_____

_____

_____

_____

_____

What am I thankful for today? _____

_____

_____

One nice thing I've done for myself today... _____

_____

_____

Day: Monday

			Carbs	Calories
Meal 1		1/2 cup 1% fat cottage cheese	5	80
		1/2 cup strawberries	6	23
Meal 2		Curves shake with 8 oz. skim milk	20	200
Meal 3		4 ounces 93% lean ground beef, broiled	0	160
		1 cup cooked carrots	11	48
		1 teaspoon butter	0	34
		Free Foods Salad		
Meal 4		2/3 cup tuna salad (recipe page 57)	4	264
		2 Rye Krisp crackers	11	60
Meal 5		8 ounces chicken breast, broiled	0	248
		1 tablespoon barbeque sauce	6	25
		1 cup Creamy Coleslaw (recipe page 60)	8	99
		1 cup steamed broccoli	5	24
		1 teaspoon butter	0	34
Meal 6		3 ounces lean ham	0	100
		1 ounce Havarti cheese	0	120

Today's Exercise:

Curves Workout ♡

or

Aerobic ♡

_____

_____

Strength Training ♡

_____

_____

Stretching ♡

_____

_____

Water: ▯ ▯ ▯ ▯ ▯ ▯ ▯ ▯
Vitamins: ⬭ ⬭ ⬭

	Carbs	Calories
Subtotals		
Minus Free Foods		
Totals for Day		

PHASE II - 3

TIP:
Check labels on ham. Some ham has a sugar cured flavoring added, which adds carbs.

*"When you have a dream
you've got to grab it and never let go."*

—*Carol Burnett*

Goals for Tuesday:

Physical: _____

_____

_____

Mental: _____

_____

_____

Spiritual: _____

_____

_____

If I had unlimited money and time, and could do anything in the world, what would it be?_____

_____

_____

_____

_____

_____

_____

What am I thankful for today? _____

_____

_____

One nice thing I've done for myself today... _____

_____

_____

_____

Day: Tuesday

		Carbs	Calories
Meal 1	2 eggs	2	150
	3 ounces ham, lean	0	100
	1 piece Holland Rusk Dry Toast	6	30
	1 teaspoon butter	0	34
Meal 2	1/2 cup cubed cantaloupe	6	25
	1/2 cup 1% fat cottage cheese	5	80
	1 ounce roasted and salted cashews	7	170
Meal 3	Greek Salad (recipe page 59)	14	383
Meal 4	Curves shake with 8 oz. skim milk	20	200
Meal 5	8 ounces broiled orange roughy	0	216
	1 cup green beans	8	40
	1 teaspoon butter	0	34
Meal 6	1 ounce Havarti cheese	0	120
	1 small apple	20	80

Water: ☐☐☐☐☐☐☐☐

Vitamins: ⬭⬭⬭

	Carbs	Calories
Subtotals		
Minus Free Foods		
Totals for Day		

Today's Exercise:

Curves Workout ♡

or

Aerobic ♡

_____
_____

Strength Training ♡

_____
_____

Stretching ♡

_____
_____

"Each friend represents a world in us, a world possibly not born until they arrive, and it is only by this meeting that a new world is born."

—Anais Nin

Goals for Wednesday:

Physical: _____

_____

_____

Mental: _____

_____

_____

Spiritual: _____

_____

_____

What are 5 things I enjoyed doing with others in the last year? _____

_____

_____

_____

_____

_____

_____

_____

What am I thankful for today? _____

_____

_____

One nice thing I've done for myself today... _____

_____

_____

Day: Wednesday

		Carbs	Calories
Meal 1	8 ounces plain yogurt	18	150
	1/4 cup blueberries	7	27
Meal 2	Curves shake with 8 oz. skim milk	20	200
Meal 3	6 ounce pork chop, broiled	0	225
	Free Foods Salad		
Meal 4	2/3 cup tuna salad (recipe page 57)	4	264
	2 Rye Krisp Crackers	11	60
Meal 5	6 ounces light smoked sausage	12	330
	1/2 cup sauerkraut	5	20
	1 cup zucchini sautééd in:	4	18
	1 tablespoon olive oil	0	120
Meal 6	3 ounces lean ham	0	100
	1 ounce Havarti cheese	0	120

Water: 🥛🥛🥛🥛🥛🥛🥛
Vitamins: ⬭ ⬭ ⬭

Subtotals		
Minus Free Foods		
Totals for Day		

Today's Exercise:

Curves Workout ♡

or

Aerobic ♡

_____

_____

Strength Training ♡

_____

_____

Stretching ♡

_____

_____

TIP:
Make sure you use a salad dressing you really enjoy. Have several on hand so you don't get bored.

PHASE II - 3

135

Nobody should seek his own good,
but the good of others.

1 Corinthians 10:24

Goals for Thursday:

Physical: _____
_____
_____

Mental: _____
_____
_____

Spiritual: _____
_____
_____

Who is the most important person in my life and why?

_____
_____
_____
_____
_____
_____
_____

What am I thankful for today? _____
_____
_____

One nice thing I've done for myself today... _____
_____
_____
_____
_____

Day: Thursday

		Carbs	Calories
Meal 1	2 eggs	2	150
	3 sausage links	0	200
	1 piece Holland Rusk Dry Toast	6	30
Meal 2	2 Keebler Harvest Bakery Multigrain crackers	11	70
	2 tablespoons vegetable cream cheese	2	90
Meal 3	Sherry-Mushroom Chicken (recipe page 66)	8	314
	1/2 cup steamed asparagus	4	22
	1 teaspoon butter	0	34
Meal 4	Curves shake with 8 oz. skim milk	20	200
Meal 5	1 serving Beef and Vegetable Stew (recipe page 62)	13	280
	Free Foods Salad		
Meal 6	1 ounce roasted and salted cashews	7	170
	1/2 cup cubed watermelon	6	25
	1 ounce cheddar cheese	0	110
	Subtotals		
	Minus Free Foods		
	Totals for Day		

Water: ⛴ ⛴ ⛴ ⛴ ⛴ ⛴ ⛴
Vitamins: ⬭ ⬭ ⬭

Today's Exercise:

Curves Workout ♡

or

Aerobic ♡

_____

_____

Strength Training ♡

_____

_____

Stretching ♡

_____

_____

PHASE II - 3

137

"Regret is an appalling waste of energy; you can't build on it; it is good only for wallowing."

—Katherine Mansfield

Goals for Friday:

Physical: _____

_____

_____

Mental: _____

_____

_____

Spiritual: _____

_____

_____

What is the biggest regret in my life? Can I do anything to change it?_____

_____

_____

_____

_____

_____

_____

_____

_____

What am I thankful for today? _____

_____

_____

One nice thing I've done for myself today... _____

_____

_____

_____

Day: Friday

		Carbs	Calories
Meal 1	2 eggs	2	150
	1 piece whole wheat bread	12	70
	1 teaspoon butter	0	34
Meal 2	Curves shake with 8 oz. skim milk	20	200
Meal 3	1 serving Easy Frittata (recipe page 64)	16	384
	Free Foods Salad		
Meal 4	1 ounce Cheddar cheese	0	110
	3 ounces lean ham	0	100
Meal 5	½ cup 1% fat cottage cheese	5	80
	½ cup cubed cantaloupe	6	25
Meal 6	2 Turkey-Lettuce Wraps (recipe page 55)	14	174

Water: 🥛🥛🥛🥛🥛🥛🥛
Vitamins: ⬭ ⬭ ⬭

	Carbs	Calories
Subtotals		
Minus Free Foods		
Totals for Day		

Today's Exercise:

Curves Workout ♡

or

Aerobic ♡

_____

_____

Strength Training ♡

_____

_____

Stretching ♡

_____

_____

PHASE II - 3

TIP:
Don't eat only iceberg lettuce, try some other varieties, it will keep your salads interesting, and keep you eating them.

*"The ultimate measure of a man is not
where he stands in moments of comfort and
convenience but where he stands at times of
challenge and controversy."*

−Martin Luther King

Goals for Saturday:

Physical: _____

_____

_____

Mental: _____

_____

_____

Spiritual: _____

_____

_____

If I could do anything in the world without fearing rejection,
what would it be? _____

_____

_____

_____

_____

_____

_____

What am I thankful for today? _____

_____

_____

One nice thing I've done for myself today... _____

_____

_____

Day: Saturday

		Carbs	Calories
Meal 1	1 slice whole wheat bread	12	70
	1 ounce Havarti cheese	0	120
	3 sausage links	0	200
Meal 2	Curves shake with 8 oz. skim milk	20	200
Meal 3	4 ounces 93% lean ground beef, broiled	0	160
	1 ounce Cheddar cheese	0	110
	1/2 cup refried beans	25	120
	2 tablespoons salsa	2	10
Meal 4	1 ounce roasted and salted cashews	7	170
	4 ounces V-8 juice	5	23
Meal 5	4 ounces broiled salmon	0	207
	Parmesan Vegetable Stir Fry (recipe page 69)	22	275
Meal 6	Free Foods Salad		

Today's Exercise:

Curves Workout ♡

or

Aerobic ♡

_____

_____

Strength Training ♡

_____

_____

Stretching ♡

_____

_____

Water: 🥛🥛🥛🥛🥛🥛🥛

Vitamins: ⬭ ⬭ ⬭

	Carbs	Calories
Subtotals		
Minus Free Foods		
Totals for Day		

"Nothing would be done at all if we waited until we could do it so well that no one could find fault with it."

–Cardinal Newman

Goals for Sunday:

Physical: _____

_____

_____

Mental: _____

_____

_____

Spiritual: _____

_____

_____

Do I procrastinate? What am I avoiding? _____

_____

_____

_____

_____

_____

_____

_____

What am I thankful for today? _____

_____

_____

One nice thing I've done for myself today... _____

_____

_____

_____

Day: Sunday

		Carbs	Calories
Meal 1	1 egg	1	75
	3 sausage links	0	200
	8 ounces V-8 juice	10	46
Meal 2	1/2 cup 1% fat cottage cheese	5	80
	1/2 cup cubed cantaloupe	6	25
Meal 3	6 ounces chicken breast, broiled	0	186
	1/2 cup snow peas	7	30
	1 teaspoon butter	0	34
	1 orange	16	65
Meal 4	1 ounce Havarti cheese	0	120
	4 ounce glass of rosé wine	6	100
Meal 5	8 ounces shrimp sautéed in:	0	240
	1 tablespoon olive oil	0	120
	1 cup spinach	2	12
	Free Foods Salad		
Meal 6	Curves shake with 8 oz. skim milk	20	200

Water: ▯▯▯▯▯▯▯▯

Vitamins: ⬭ ⬭ ⬭

	Carbs	Calories
Subtotals		
Minus Free Foods		
Totals for Day		

Today's Exercise:

Curves Workout ♡

or

Aerobic ♡

_____

_____

Strength Training ♡

_____

_____

Stretching ♡

_____

_____

LOOKING AHEAD

Tomorrow you need to go to Curves to be weighed and have your body fat tested. Record your results here:

Weight_____

% Body Fat _____

Pounds of
Body Fat _____

Also record your results on the chart on page 7.

PHASE II - 3

143

SHOPPING LIST–PHASE II, WEEK 4

Vegetables
____1 cup asparagus
____1 cup broccoli florets
____1 cup carrots
____1 cup cauliflower florets
____1 stalk celery
____$1/2$ cup whole kernel corn
____1 green onion
____1 radish
____$1/2$ cup snow peas
____1 cup spinach, fresh
____1 cup zucchini, sliced

_____
_____
_____

Free Foods
____enough for 6 salads

Dairy
____1 tablespoon blue cheese, crumbled
____3 tablespoons butter
____5 ounces Cheddar cheese
____2 cups cottage cheese, lowfat (1%), small curd
____7 eggs
____5 ounces Monterey Jack cheese
____ $1/2$ gallon milk, skim
____2 tablespoons vegetable cream cheese
____8 ounces yogurt, plain, lowfat

_____
_____
_____

Fruit
____1 small apple
____$1/4$ cup blueberries
____$1^1/2$ cup cantaloupe, cubed
____1 small orange
____1 cup strawberries
____1 cup watermelon, cubed

_____

_____
_____
_____
_____

Meat
____1 (6-ounce) can solid white albacore tuna, packed in water
____10 ounces ground beef, 93% lean (divided)
____12 ounces chicken breast
____12 ounces ham, lean
____6-ounce pork chop, lean
____8 ounces orange roughy
____4 ounces salmon
____9 breakfast sausage links
____8 ounces shrimp

_____
_____
_____
_____

Starches
____1 piece Holland Rusk Dry Toast
____2 Keebler Harvest Bakery Multigrain crackers
____6 Rye Krisp crackers
____1 slice whole wheat bread

_____
_____
_____

Other
____2 ounces dry roasted peanuts
____$1/2$ cup refried beans
____2 tablespoons salsa
____12 ounces V-8 juice
____8 ounces rosé wine

_____
_____
_____
_____

PHASE II - 3

PHASE II

~ WEEK 4 ~

*As long as you are losing at least 1 pound per week you should continue on Phase II.
If your weight loss drops below 1 pound per week during Phase II,
you should move to Phase III.*

~

HIGHER PROTEIN/LOW CARBOHYDRATE

For the higher protein/low carbohydrate version, you should:

Enjoy unlimited amounts of lean meats, cheeses, eggs, seafood and poultry
(baked, broiled, or boiled—never fried).

Eat moderate to lower amounts of fat.
Limit your carbohydrate intake to 40-60 grams per day
(after subtracting free foods).

Eat, but don't cheat!

CALORIE-RESTRICTED

For the calorie-restricted version, you should:

Eat no more than 1600 calories per day
(after subtracting free foods).

Consume 40% of those calories in the form of protein foods.

Consume no more than 60 grams of carbohydrates per day
(after subtracting free foods).

~

HINT: Circle or highlight free foods in your food diary, so that you can easily subtract them from the totals. See page 39 for an example.

ANOTHER HINT: You are not required to eat the meals in the order they are listed. Feel free to adjust them to your lifestyle and schedule.

PHASE II - 4

NEEDS

List 5 foods you feel you cannot live without:

1. _____
2. _____
3. _____
4. _____
5. _____

List 3 foods that calm you down:

1. _____
2. _____
3. _____

List 3 foods that make you happy:

1. _____
2. _____
3. _____

Dr. Abraham Maslow created a model of our Hierarchy Of Needs, which describes how we prioritize. Our first priority is always our biological needs. This is good because it ensures the survival of our species. The next priority is for our safety, also vital to our survival. If both of these needs are being satisfied, then we may move on to our need for attachment to others. After that comes our need for esteem, and then our need to have a meaningful existence, also called self-actualization.

Our subconscious minds drive us to eat certain foods or quantities of food. Our food choices should meet our biological needs, and should not be driven by our subconscious. Our needs for security and self-esteem cannot really be taken care of by eating chocolate, and 5,000 calories every day will never satisfy our need to be loved.

PHASE II - 4

WANTS

Giving in to every desire is immature behavior, and will ultimately bring some bad consequence. It is important to be able to tell the difference between genuine needs (are you hungry?) and momentary wants (would you love to munch on a bag of potato chips?). Some women find that they must remove themselves from the presence of the desired food to keep from eating it. Don't feel silly if you have to do this—there is no shame in using your self control to avoid doing something you will regret later.

If cravings are a continual problem for you, maybe you need to examine the situations and people involved. You might start a cravings journal and take note of where you were, what time of the day it was, who was with you, and how you were feeling otherwise. This should not give you an excuse to overeat after every tense meeting, it should help to give you insight into your own thinking and help you to control yourself.

What are you craving right now?

_____

_____

_____

What will happen if you don't give in?

_____

_____

_____

What will happen if you do give in?

_____

_____

_____

Which consequence is more attractive to you?

_____

What will it take to let this craving pass by?

_____

_____

PHASE II - 4

147

*"Wonderful things start to happen when
you dream outside of your sleep."*

— Richard Wilkins

Goals for Monday:

Physical: _____
_____
_____

Mental: _____
_____
_____

Spiritual: _____
_____
_____

What is the one dream for my life I am most eager to
achieve? _____
_____
_____
_____
_____
_____
_____

What am I thankful for today? _____
_____
_____

One nice thing I've done for myself today... _____
_____
_____
_____

Day: Monday

		Carbs	Calories
Meal 1	½ cup 1% fat cottage cheese	5	80
	½ cup strawberries	6	23
Meal 2	Curves shake with 8 oz. skim milk	20	200
Meal 3	6 ounces 93% lean ground beef, broiled	0	240
	1 cup cooked carrots	12	48
	1 teaspoon butter	0	34
Meal 4	⅔ cup tuna salad (recipe page 57)	4	264
	2 Rye Krisp crackers	11	60
Meal 5	1 serving Spicy Chili Pork Chops (recipe page 65)	4	219
	1 cup steamed cauliflower	5	26
	1 teaspoon butter	0	34
	Free Foods Salad		
Meal 6	3 ounces lean ham	0	100
	1 ounce Monterey Jack cheese	0	110
	4-ounce glass of rosé wine	6	100

Water: ⊔ ⊔ ⊔ ⊔ ⊔ ⊔ ⊔

Vitamins: ⊂⊃ ⊂⊃ ⊂⊃

	Carbs	Calories
Subtotals		
Minus Free Foods		
Totals for Day		

Today's Exercise:

Curves Workout ♡

or

Aerobic ♡

_____

_____

Strength Training ♡

_____

_____

Stretching ♡

_____

_____

TIP:
Try some of the Curves shake variations (page 37) so you don't get bored.

PHASE II - 4

But when you pray, go into your room,
close the door and pray to your Father,
who is unseen. Then your Father, who sees
what is done in secret, will reward you.

Matthew 6:6

Goals for Tuesday:

Physical: _____

_____

_____

Mental: _____

_____

Spiritual: _____

_____

_____

What are 5 things I enjoyed doing alone in the last year?

_____

_____

_____

_____

_____

_____

What am I thankful for today? _____

_____

_____

One nice thing I've done for myself today... _____

_____

_____

_____

Day: Tuesday

		Carbs	Calories
Meal 1	2 eggs	2	150
	3 ounces lean ham	0	100
	1 teaspoon butter (for cooking eggs and ham)	0	34
Meal 2	½ cup cubed cantaloupe	6	25
	½ cup 1% fat cottage cheese	5	80
Meal 3	Greek Salad (recipe page 59)	14	383
Meal 4	Curves shake with 8 oz. skim milk	20	200
Meal 5	1 serving Jamaican Seafood Medley		
	(recipe page 67)	7	287
	½ cup whole kernel corn	13	66
	1 cup zucchini sautéed in:	4	18
	1 tablespoon olive oil	0	120
Meal 6	1 ounce Cheddar cheese	0	110
	1 small apple	20	80
	Subtotals		
	Minus Free Foods		
	Totals for Day		

Water: ⊡ ⊡ ⊡ ⊡ ⊡ ⊡ ⊡ ⊡

Vitamins: ⊂⊃ ⊂⊃ ⊂⊃

Today's Exercise:

Curves Workout ♡

or

Aerobic ♡

_____

_____

Strength Training ♡

_____

_____

Stretching ♡

_____

_____

PHASE II - 4

151

"He who accepts the unaltered philosophy of another is as ludicrous as he who dons his neighbor's hat, and infinitely more ridiculous."

— Paulette Goddard

Goals for Wednesday:

Physical: _____

_____

_____

Mental: _____

_____

_____

Spiritual: _____

_____

_____

What is my philosophy of life? _____

_____

_____

_____

_____

_____

What am I thankful for today? _____

_____

_____

One nice thing I've done for myself today... _____

_____

_____

_____

_____

Day: Wednesday

		Carbs	Calories
Meal 1	8 ounces plain yogurt	18	150
	1/4 cup blueberries	7	27
Meal 2	Curves shake with 8 oz. skim milk	20	200
Meal 3	6 ounce pork chop, broiled	0	225
	Spinach Salad (recipe page 58)		
	with 2 tablespoons Orange Vinaigrette	11	138
Meal 4	1 serving Italian Stuffed Mushrooms		
	(recipe page 56)	16	192
	8 ounces V-8 juice	10	46
Meal 5	1 serving Beef Tenderloin with Blue Cheese	1	383
	(recipe page 63)		
	Free Foods Salad		
Meal 6	3 ounces ham, lean	0	100
	1 ounce Monterey Jack cheese	0	110

Water: ▢▢▢▢▢▢▢

Vitamins: ⬭⬭⬭

Subtotals		
Minus Free Foods		
Totals for Day		

Today's Exercise:

Curves Workout ♡

or

Aerobic ♡

_____

_____

Strength Training ♡

_____

_____

Stretching ♡

_____

_____

TIP:
When someone says "it's too bad you can't eat this," reply "I could eat it, but I choose not to." Take responsibility for your choices.

PHASE II - 4

153

Each one should test his own actions.
Then he can take pride in himself without
comparing himself to somebody else, for
each one should carry his own load.

Galatians 6:8

Goals for Thursday:

Physical: _____

_____

Mental: _____

_____

Spiritual: _____

_____

What are 5 things I accomplished in the last year? _____

_____

_____

_____

_____

_____

What am I thankful for today? _____

_____

_____

One nice thing I've done for myself today... _____

_____

_____

Day: Thursday

		Carbs	Calories
Meal 1	2 eggs	2	150
	3 sausage links	0	200
	1 piece Holland Rusk Dry Toast	6	30
Meal 2	2 Keebler Harvest Bakery Multigrain crackers	11	70
	2 tablespoons vegetable cream cheese	2	90
	1 cup cubed watermelon	12	50
Meal 3	6 ounces chicken breast, broiled	0	186
	1 tablespoon blue cheese (melted on chicken)	0	30
	1 cup steamed broccoli	5	24
	1 teaspoon butter	0	34
Meal 4	Curves shake with 8 oz. skim milk	20	200
Meal 5	1 serving Beef and Vegetable Stew (recipe page 62)	13	280
	Free Foods Salad		
Meal 6	1 ounce dry roasted peanuts	5	160
	1 ounce Cheddar cheese	0	110

Today's Exercise:

Curves Workout ♡

or

Aerobic ♡

_____

_____

Strength Training ♡

_____

_____

Stretching ♡

_____

_____

Water: 🥛🥛🥛🥛🥛🥛🥛🥛

Vitamins: ⬭ ⬭ ⬭

	Carbs	Calories
Subtotals		
Minus Free Foods		
Totals for Day		

...a time to be born and a time to die, a time to plant and a time to uproot, a time to kill and a time to heal, a time to tear down and a time to build...

Ecclesiastes 3:2-3

Goals for Friday:

Physical: _____
_____
_____

Mental: _____
_____
_____

Spiritual: _____
_____
_____

Am I most comfortable when everything around me stays exactly the same? _____
_____
_____
_____
_____
_____

What am I thankful for today? _____
_____
_____

One nice thing I've done for myself today... _____
_____
_____
_____

Day: Friday

		Carbs	Calories
Meal 1	2 eggs	2	150
	3 ounces ham	0	100
	1 teaspoon butter (for cooking eggs and ham)	0	34
Meal 2	Curves shake with 8 oz. skim milk	20	200
Meal 3	2 Turkey-Lettuce Wraps (recipe page 55)	14	174
	½ cup strawberries	6	23
Meal 4	2 ounces Cheddar cheese	0	220
	2 Rye Krisp crackers	11	60
Meal 5	8 ounces shrimp sautéed in:	0	240
	1 tablespoon olive oil	0	120
	1 cup steamed asparagus	8	44
	1 teaspoon butter	0	34
	Free Foods Salad		
Meal 6	½ cup 1% fat cottage cheese	5	80
	½ cup cubed cantaloupe	6	25

Water: 🥛🥛🥛🥛🥛🥛🥛
Vitamins: ⬭ ⬭ ⬭

	Carbs	Calories
Subtotals		
Minus Free Foods		
Totals for Day		

Today's Exercise:

Curves Workout ♡

or

Aerobic ♡

_____

_____

Strength Training ♡

_____

_____

Stretching ♡

_____

_____

TIP:
Try melting your cheese on Rye-Krisp crackers. You can do it quickly in the microwave. Many cheeses taste quite different when melted.

PHASE II - 4

157

"Inaction saps the vigor of the mind."

—Leonardo da Vinci

Goals for Saturday:

Physical: _____

_____

_____

Mental: _____

_____

_____

Spiritual: _____

_____

_____

How many hours per week do I watch TV? Am I really enjoying it or am I doing it because of habit? _____

_____

_____

_____

_____

_____

_____

_____

What am I thankful for today? _____

_____

_____

One nice thing I've done for myself today... _____

_____

_____

_____

_____

Day: Saturday

			Carbs	Calories
Meal 1		1 slice whole wheat bread	12	70
		1 ounce Monterey Jack cheese	0	110
		3 sausage links	0	200
Meal 2		Curves shake with 8 oz. skim milk	20	200
Meal 3		4 ounces 93% lean ground beef, broiled	0	160
		1 ounce Cheddar cheese	0	110
		1/2 cup refried beans	25	120
		2 tablespoons salsa	2	10
Meal 4		4 ounces broiled salmon	0	207
		1 serving Spicy Zucchini Boats (page 54)	5	210
Meal 5		Free Foods Salad		
Meal 6		1 ounce dry roasted peanuts	5	160
		4 ounces V-8 juice	5	25

Today's Exercise:

Curves Workout ♡

or

Aerobic ♡

_____

_____

Strength Training ♡

_____

_____

Stretching ♡

_____

_____

Water: 🥛🥛🥛🥛🥛🥛🥛🥛

Vitamins: ⬭ ⬭ ⬭

Subtotals	
Minus Free Foods	
Totals for Day	

A fool gives full vent to his anger, but
a wise man keeps himself under control.

Proverbs 29:11

Goals for Sunday:

Physical: _____

_____

_____

Mental: _____

_____

_____

Spiritual: _____

_____

_____

Who or what has the capacity to make me the most angry?

_____

_____

_____

_____

_____

_____

What am I thankful for today? _____

_____

_____

One nice thing I've done for myself today... _____

_____

_____

_____

Day: Sunday

			Carbs	Calories
Meal 1	1 egg		1	75
	3 sausage links		0	200
Meal 2	½ cup 1% fat cottage cheese		5	80
	½ cup cubed cantaloupe		6	25
Meal 3	6 ounces chicken breast, broiled		0	186
	½ cup snow peas		7	30
	1 teaspoon butter		0	34
	1 orange		16	65
Meal 4	2 ounces Monterey Jack cheese		0	220
	2 Rye Krisp crackers		11	60
	4 ounce glass of rosé wine		6	100
Meal 5	8 ounces orange roughy sautéed in:		0	216
	1 tablespoon olive oil		0	120
	1 cup spinach		2	12
	Free Foods Salad			
Meal 6	Curves shake with 8 oz. skim milk		20	200

Water: 🥛🥛🥛🥛🥛🥛🥛
Vitamins: 💊💊💊

	Carbs	Calories
Subtotals		
Minus Free Foods		
Totals for Day		

Today's Exercise:

Curves Workout ♡

or

Aerobic ♡

_____

_____

Strength Training ♡

_____

_____

Stretching ♡

_____

_____

LOOKING AHEAD

Tomorrow you need to go to Curves to be weighed and have your body fat tested. Record your results here:

Weight_____
% Body Fat _____

Pounds of
Body Fat _____

Also record your results on the chart on page 7.

PHASE II - 4

161

SHOPPING LIST–PHASE II, WEEK 5

Vegetables
____$^1/_2$ cup baby carrots
____$2^1/_2$ cups broccoli florets
____1 cup cauliflower florets
____1 stalk celery
____1 cup green beans
____1 green onion
____$^1/_2$ cup mushrooms, sliced
____1 green onion
____1 radish
____$^1/_2$ cup snow peas
____1 cup zucchini, sliced

_____
_____
_____
_____
_____

Free Foods
____enough for 6 salads

Dairy
____4 tablespoons butter
____1 tablespoon blue cheese
____4 ounces Cheddar cheese
____2 cups cottage cheese, lowfat (1%), small curd
____6 eggs
____$^1/_2$ gallon milk, skim
____5 ounces Swiss cheese
____2 tablespoons vegetable cream cheese
____4 ounces yogurt, plain, lowfat

_____
_____
_____

Fruit
____$^1/_2$ cup seedless grapes
____$1^3/_4$ cups strawberries
____$1^1/_2$ cups watermelon, cubed

_____
_____
_____
_____

Meat
____8 slices bacon
____16 ounces chicken breast
____14 ounces ground beef, 93% lean (divided)
____3 ounces ham, lean
____6-ounce pork chop, lean
____2 ounces deli roast beef
____6 ounces salmon
____6-ounce sirloin steak, well trimmed
____6 breakfast sausage links
____8 ounces light smoked sausage
____8 ounces shrimp
____1 (6-ounce) can solid white albacore tuna, packed in water
____2 ounces deli turkey breast

_____
_____

Starches
____4 Rye Krisp crackers
____4 Keebler Harvest Bakery Multigrain crackers
____3 slices whole wheat bread

_____
_____

Other
____2 ounces roasted and salted almonds
____1 tablespoon barbeque sauce
____$^1/_2$ cup French vanilla ice cream
____2 ounces pistachio nuts (in shells)
____1 ounce dry roasted peanuts
____$^1/_2$ cup refried beans
____2 tablespoons salsa
____$^1/_2$ cup sauerkraut
____4 ounces V-8 juice
____4 ounces rosé wine

_____
_____

PHASE II

~ WEEK 5 ~

*If your weight loss drops below 1 pound per week
during Phase II, you should move to Phase III.
If you have reached your goal weight, you should move to Phase III.*

~

HIGHER PROTEIN/LOW CARBOHYDRATE

For the higher protein/low carbohydrate version, you should:

Enjoy unlimited amounts of lean meats, cheeses, eggs, seafood and poultry
(baked, broiled, or boiled—never fried).

Eat moderate to lower amounts of fat.
Limit your carbohydrate intake to 40-60 grams per day
(after subtracting free foods).

Eat, but don't cheat!

CALORIE-RESTRICTED

For the calorie-restricted version, you should:

Eat no more than 1600 calories per day
(after subtracting free foods).

Consume 40% of those calories in the form of protein foods.

Consume no more than 60 grams of carbohydrates per day
(after subtracting free foods).

~

HINT: Circle or highlight free foods in your food diary, so that you can
easily subtract them from the totals. See page 39 for an example.

ANOTHER HINT: You are not required to eat the meals in the order they
are listed. Feel free to adjust them to your lifestyle and schedule.

Weekly Lesson #6

~

PERMANENT RESULTS

List 3 things that are different about you since starting this 6 week challenge:

1. _____
2. _____
3. _____

List 5 foods you have truly enjoyed eating during the last 5 weeks on the plan:

1. _____
2. _____
3. _____
4. _____
5. _____

List 3 things that will be difficult about Phase III:

1. _____
2. _____
3. _____

Even if you have only lost 5 pounds over the last 5 weeks, you want to maintain that weight loss. If you have reached your goal weight, you certainly don't want to gain the weight back. Thankfully, the Curves Weight Loss Method gives us a way to eat normally most of the time and still maintain our weight. Phase III allows us to raise our metabolism to pre-dieting levels without gaining weight back to pre-diet levels.

Be aware that following Phase III is an entirely different discipline than following Phases I and II. You must weigh yourself EVERY day, at approximately the same time of day, in approximately the same circumstances. You must be prepared to do 3 days of the Phase I plan whenever you reach your "high" weight. Be sure that you eat an adequate amount and a variety of food. You will be able to eat normally and yet maintain a healthy weight.

LOOKING BACK

Think back to when you began this 6 week challenge. You have made gains in many areas of your life. You may have attained your goal weight and body fat percentage, or you may have more to accomplish. In either case, you are to be congratulated for your courage and perseverance. You have voluntarily denied yourself the short term pleasure of eating whatever you want whenever you want. You have willingly taken the time to exercise and to plan your eating. You have become comfortable with being a little bit uncomfortable.

Now you know how to follow the Curves Weight Loss Method and allow yourself to achieve Permanent Results Without Permanent Dieting. The rest is up to you. You are armed with experience and knowledge, but you will still have to choose correctly every day.

You can do it!

Name 3 things about this plan that at first seemed difficult but now seem easy:

1._____
2._____
3._____

Name 2 things about this plan that never did get to be easy:

1._____
2._____

List 6 reasons to maintain your weight loss:

1._____
2._____
3._____
4._____
5._____
6._____

*"The poor man is not he who is without a cent,
but he who is without a dream."*

—Harry Kemp

Goals for Monday:

Physical: _____
_____
_____

Mental: _____
_____
_____

Spiritual: _____
_____
_____

What are 10 things I want to do before I die?_____
_____
_____
_____
_____
_____
_____
_____
_____
_____
_____

What am I thankful for today? _____
_____
_____

One nice thing I've done for myself today... _____
_____

Day: <u>Monday</u>

		Carbs	Calories
Meal 1	2 ounces deli turkey breast	2	60
	1 ounce Swiss cheese	0	110
	1 piece whole wheat bread	12	70
	1 tablespoon light mayonnaise	1	50
Meal 2	½ cup 1% fat cottage cheese	5	80
	½ cup baby carrots	5	24
Meal 3	4 ounces 93% lean ground beef, broiled	0	160
	1 cup French Onion Soup (recipe page 61)	15	199
Meal 4	⅔ cup tuna salad (recipe page 57)	4	264
	2 Rye Krisp crackers	11	60
Meal 5	1 serving Spicy Chili Pork Chops (recipe page 65)	4	219
	1 cup steamed broccoli	5	24
	1 teaspoon butter	0	34
	Free Foods Salad		
Meal 6	Curves shake with 8 oz. skim milk	20	200
	Subtotals		
Water: 🥛🥛🥛🥛🥛🥛🥛🥛	**Minus Free Foods**		
Vitamins: ⬭ ⬭ ⬭	**Totals for Day**		

Today's Exercise:

Curves Workout ♡

or

Aerobic ♡

_____

_____

Strength Training ♡

_____

_____

Stretching ♡

_____

_____

TIP:
Eating out got you stumped? See page 34 for some hints.

*So we make it our goal to please him, whether
we are at home in the body or away from it.*

2 Corinthians 5:9

Goals for Tuesday:

Physical: _____

_____

_____

Mental: _____

_____

_____

Spiritual: _____

_____

_____

What are my goals in life? For the next year? 5 years?
20 years? _____

_____

_____

_____

_____

_____

_____

_____

What am I thankful for today? _____

_____

_____

One nice thing I've done for myself today... _____

_____

_____

Day: <u>Tuesday</u>

		Carbs	Calories
Meal 1	1 egg	1	75
	3 ounces lean ham	0	100
Meal 2	½ cup strawberries	6	23
	½ cup 1% fat cottage cheese	5	80
Meal 3	4 ounces chicken breast, broiled	0	124
	Spinach Salad (recipe page 58)		
	with 2 tablespoons Orange Vinaigrette	11	138
	1 piece whole wheat bread	12	70
	½ tablespoon butter	0	51
Meal 4	Curves shake with 8 oz. skim milk	20	200
Meal 5	1 serving Jamaican Seafood Medley (recipe page 67)	7	287
	1 cup zucchini sautéed in:	4	18
	1 tablespoon olive oil	0	120
	1 serving Frozen Chocolate Mousse (recipe page 70)	9	127
Meal 6	1 ounce Cheddar cheese	0	110
	½ cup seedless grapes	14	57
	1 ounce roasted and salted almonds	4	180
	Subtotals		
	Minus Free Foods		
	Totals for Day		

Water: ⛾ ⛾ ⛾ ⛾ ⛾ ⛾ ⛾

Vitamins: ⬭ ⬭ ⬭

Today's Exercise:

Curves Workout ♡

or

Aerobic ♡

_____

_____

Strength Training ♡

_____

_____

Stretching ♡

_____

_____

Are you so foolish? After beginning with the Spirit, are you now trying to attain your goal by human effort?

Galatians 3:3

Goals for Wednesday:

Physical: _____
_____
_____

Mental: _____
_____
_____

Spiritual: _____
_____
_____

Look back at the goals I set for myself on page 76. How did I do? How realistic were my goals? _____
_____
_____
_____
_____
_____
_____

What am I thankful for today? _____
_____
_____

One nice thing I've done for myself today... _____
_____
_____
_____

Day: <u>Wednesday</u>

		Carbs	Calories
Meal 1	4 ounces plain yogurt	9	75
	1/4 cup strawberries	6	23
Meal 2	Curves shake with 8 oz. skim milk	20	200
Meal 3	6 ounces lean ground beef, broiled	0	240
	1/2 cup refried beans	25	120
	1 ounce Cheddar cheese	0	110
	2 tablespoon salsa	2	10
Meal 4	1 serving Italian Stuffed Mushrooms (recipe page 56)	16	192
Meal 5	6 ounce pork chop, broiled	0	225
	Free Foods Salad		
Meal 6	2 ounces deli roast beef	2	60
	1 ounce Swiss cheese	0	110

Water: 🥛🥛🥛🥛🥛🥛🥛
Vitamins: ⬯ ⬯ ⬯

	Carbs	Calories
Subtotals		
Minus Free Foods		
Totals for Day		

Today's Exercise:

Curves Workout ♡

or

Aerobic ♡

_____
_____

Strength Training ♡

_____
_____

Stretching ♡

_____
_____

TIP:
Even if you consider yourself a pro at estimating food portions, it is smart to actually measure them whenever possible.

171

"There are only two things that prevent you from accomplishing your goals—fear and self doubt. When you learn to trust yourself and ask for help, the world gets a whole lot easier."

—Wyatt Webb

Goals for Thursday:

Physical: _____

_____

Mental: _____

_____

Spiritual: _____

_____

What is one thing I can do in five minutes to make today simpler? (i.e. return phone calls, clean off desk, pay some bills, file papers) _____

_____

_____

_____

_____

_____

What am I thankful for today? _____

_____

One nice thing I've done for myself today... _____

_____

Day: Thursday

		Carbs	Calories
Meal 1	2 eggs	2	150
	4 slices bacon	0	120
	4 ounces V-8 juice	5	23
Meal 2	2 Harvest Bakery Multigrain crackers	11	70
	2 tablespoons vegetable cream cheese	2	90
	1 cup cubed watermelon	12	50
Meal 3	6 ounces chicken breast, broiled	0	186
	1 tablespoon blue cheese (melted on chicken)	0	30
	1 cup steamed broccoli	5	24
	1 teaspoon butter	0	34
Meal 4	Curves shake with 8 oz. skim milk	20	200
Meal 5	6 ounces sirloin steak, broiled	0	323
	Free Foods Salad		
Meal 6	1 ounce roasted and salted almonds	4	180
	1 ounce Cheddar cheese	0	110
	4 ounce glass of rosé wine	6	100
	Subtotals		
	Minus Free Foods		
	Totals for Day		

Water: ⬜⬜⬜⬜⬜⬜⬜

Vitamins: ⬭ ⬭ ⬭

Today's Exercise:

Curves Workout ♡

or

Aerobic ♡

_____

_____

Strength Training ♡

_____

_____

Stretching ♡

_____

_____

173

"The greater part of our happiness or misery depends on our dispositions, and not on our circumstances."
—Martha Washington

Goals for Friday:

Physical: _____

_____

Mental: _____

_____

Spiritual: _____

_____

What 3 things do I like about myself? _____

_____

_____

_____

_____

_____

What am I thankful for today? _____

_____

_____

One nice thing I've done for myself today... _____

_____

_____

_____

Day: <u>Friday</u>

		Carbs	Calories
Meal 1	1 egg	1	75
	3 sausage links	0	200
Meal 2	Curves shake with 8 oz. skim milk	20	200
Meal 3	4 ounces lean ground beef, broiled	0	160
	1 tablespoon barbeque sauce	6	25
	1/2 cup Creamy Coleslaw (recipe page 60)	8	99
Meal 4	1 ounce Swiss cheese	0	110
	2 Rye Krisp crackers	11	60
	2 ounces pistachio nuts (in shells)	7	170
Meal 5	8 ounces shrimp sautéed in:	0	240
	1 tablespoon olive oil	0	120
	1 cup steamed cauliflower	5	26
	1 teaspoon butter	0	34
	Free Foods Salad		
Meal 6	1/2 cup 1% fat cottage cheese	5	80
	1/2 cup strawberries	6	23

Water: ⊔ ⊔ ⊔ ⊔ ⊔ ⊔ ⊔ ⊔

Vitamins: ⊂⊃ ⊂⊃ ⊂⊃

	Carbs	Calories
Subtotals		
Minus Free Foods		
Totals for Day		

Today's Exercise:

Curves Workout ♡

or

Aerobic ♡

_____

_____

Strength Training ♡

_____

_____

Stretching ♡

_____

_____

TIP:
You need to reward yourself for making it to this point. How about a facial or a massage or a manicure?

175

But I have prayed for you,...that your faith may not fail. And when you have turned back, strengthen your brothers.

Luke 22:32

Goals for Saturday:

Physical: _____

_____

_____

Mental: _____

_____

_____

Spiritual: _____

_____

_____

Name the 3 most difficult challenges of this diet. What can I do to improve in these areas? _____

_____

_____

_____

_____

_____

_____

What am I thankful for today? _____

_____

_____

One nice thing I've done for myself today... _____

_____

_____

_____

Day: Saturday

		Carbs	Calories
Meal 1	1 slice whole wheat bread	12	70
	1 ounce Cheddar cheese	0	110
	3 sausage links	0	200
Meal 2	Curves shake with 8 oz. skim milk	20	200
Meal 3	Free Foods Salad		
Meal 4	6 ounces chicken breast, broiled	0	186
	1/2 cup snow peas	7	30
	1 teaspoon butter	0	34
Meal 5	6 ounces broiled salmon	0	311
	Stir fry of:		
	1 tablespoon olive oil	0	120
	1/2 cup onion	7	30
	1/2 cup mushrooms	4	21
	1/2 cup broccoli	3	12
Meal 6	1/2 cup French vanilla ice cream	15	160
	1/2 cup strawberries	6	23
	1 ounce dry roasted peanuts	5	160

Water: ⬚ ⬚ ⬚ ⬚ ⬚ ⬚ ⬚

Vitamins: ⬚ ⬚ ⬚

	Carbs	Calories
Subtotals		
Minus Free Foods		
Totals for Day		

Today's Exercise:

Curves Workout ♡

or

Aerobic ♡

_____

_____

Strength Training ♡

_____

_____

Stretching ♡

_____

_____

If you are still losing 1 to 2 pounds per week, you should continue doing Phase II. When you reach your goal weight or a plateau, go to Phase III (page 181)

*"Strength is the capacity to break a chocolate bar
into four pieces with your bare hands—
and then eat just one of the pieces."*

—Judith Viorst

Goals for Sunday:

Physical: _____

_____

_____

Mental: _____

_____

_____

Spiritual: _____

_____

_____

Name 3 positive behavioral changes I have made during this
diet. _____

_____

_____

_____

_____

_____

What am I thankful for today? _____

_____

_____

One nice thing I've done for myself today... _____

_____

_____

_____

Day: Sunday

		Carbs	Calories
Meal 1	2 eggs	2	150
	4 slices bacon	0	120
Meal 2	¹/₂ cup 1% fat cottage cheese	5	80
	¹/₂ cup cubed watermelon	6	25
Meal 3	8 ounces light smoked sausage	16	440
	¹/₂ cup sauerkraut	5	20
	1 cup green beans	8	40
	1 teaspoon butter	0	34
Meal 4	2 ounces Swiss cheese	0	220
	2 Keebler Harvest Bakery Multigrain crackers	11	70
Meal 5	Sherry-Mushroom Chicken (recipe page 66)	8	314
	Free Foods Salad		
Meal 6	Curves shake with 8 oz. skim milk	20	200

Water: ▯ ▯ ▯ ▯ ▯ ▯ ▯
Vitamins: ▭ ▭ ▭

Subtotals		
Minus Free Foods		
Totals for Day		

Today's Exercise:

Curves Workout ♡

or

Aerobic ♡

_____

_____

Strength Training ♡

_____

_____

Stretching ♡

_____

_____

LOOKING AHEAD

Tomorrow you need to go to Curves to be weighed, measured and have your body fat tested. Record your results here:

Weight_____

% Body Fat_____

Pounds of Body Fat _____

Record your results on the chart on page 7. You also need to have measurements taken and recorded in the chart on page 6 (Week 6 Measurements)

179

"The longer I live, the more I realize
the impact of attitude on life.
Attitude, to me, is more important than
education, than money, than circumstances,
than failures, than successes, than appearance,
giftedness or skill. It will make or break
a company, church or home.
The remarkable thing is that we have
a choice every day regarding the attitude
we will embrace for that day.
We cannot change our past.
We cannot change the fact that
people will act in a certain way.
We cannot change the inevitable.
The only thing we can do is play on the one
string we have, and that is our attitude.
I am convinced that life is
10% of what happens to me
and 90% how I react to it.
And so it is with you.
We are in charge of our attitudes."

–Charles Swindoll

PHASE III

*If you have more weight to lose and you are still losing
1 to 2 pounds per week, you may stay on Phase II until you
either reach your goal or you hit a plateau.*

~

You should begin Phase III if:

* You have reached your goal

* You have hit a plateau

* You are ready to take a break from dieting

~

Phase III is not really a diet, it is mostly eating.
The objective is to raise your metabolism back to pre-diet levels
without regaining the weight you lost.

The objective of Phase III is to raise metabolism back up to the level it was before you began this diet. Phase III is not really a diet; in fact, it is mostly eating. Eating is what stops the production of starvation hormones and raises metabolism.

Because your metabolic rate has decreased due to dieting, you will gain weight from eating more calories than you are burning. The first couple of pounds that you immediately gain after going off a diet are water weight. Because you no longer need to access stored energy (body fat), your body will rehydrate. The key is to not gain more weight than you can lose in a 72-hour period (3 days), because that's how long it takes for your body to begin producing starvation hormones. You must also continue to exercise at least 3 days per week to keep your metabolism high and to encourage your body to preserve its muscle mass.

PHASE III MAINTENANCE CHART EXAMPLE

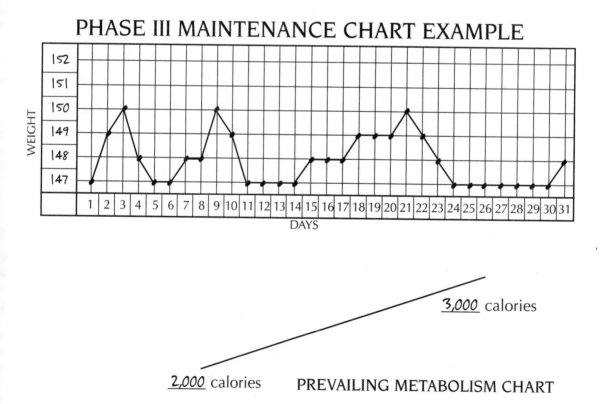

SUCCESS!

You have reached your goal weight and want to maintain it. Establish a low weight (your current weight) and a high weight (3-5 pounds over that). Now you must begin eating normally (2000-3000 calories per day) and you must weigh yourself every day. You will probably gain 1-2 pounds in the first day or two.

When the scale registers at the high weight, you will need to do the Phase I diet for 2-3 days, until you are back at the low weight. The 3-5 pounds you will gain probably consist of 2-3 pounds of water and 1 pound of body fat. The Phase I diet will cause you to dehydrate and burn off the body fat that you gained. Because you only do the Phase I diet for 2-3 days, you won't restimulate the production of starvation hormones. You must be sure to eat an adequate amount of food for your body size and activity level; this is the only way to raise your metabolism. Most importantly, you must never gain more weight than you can lose in 2-3 days.

Your goal is to be able to eat normally for about 29 days a month and need to diet for 2-3 days a month. The following chart will help you monitor the Phase III process. (See page 182 for an example of how to use the chart.) Record your low weight (your current weight) and your high weight (3-5 pounds more) on the left side, going up in pounds. The bottom of the chart marks off days. Start with Day 1 and make a dot at your weight. Move along the chart, following the Phase III plan by dieting when you must and eating normally otherwise. Notice that over a period of time, it will take longer and longer to gain that 3-5 pounds, so you will have more days of eating normally. You will know your prevailing metabolism by the amount of food that you can eat without gaining weight.

PHASE III MAINTENANCE CHART

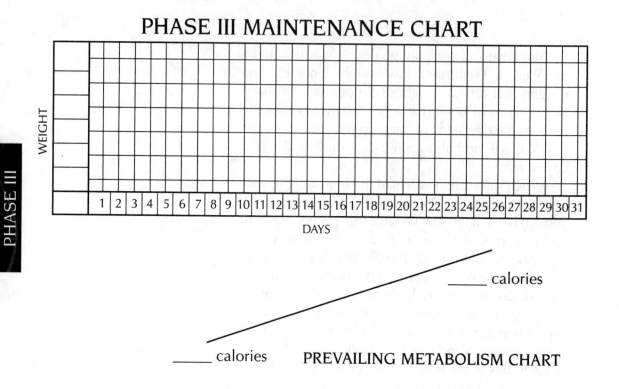

WEIGHT

| | 1 | 2 | 3 | 4 | 5 | 6 | 7 | 8 | 9 | 10 | 11 | 12 | 13 | 14 | 15 | 16 | 17 | 18 | 19 | 20 | 21 | 22 | 23 | 24 | 25 | 26 | 27 | 28 | 29 | 30 | 31 |

DAYS

_____ calories

_____ calories   PREVAILING METABOLISM CHART

MORE TO GO

You have been losing weight, but have reached a plateau and just can't seem to lose any more weight, even though you are following the Phase II plan faithfully. There is no reason to continue to diet; it is time to raise your metabolism. You need to enjoy Phase III for a month or two. This will be a time to eat healthfully and abundantly. You will raise your metabolism back to its pre-dieting level without regaining the weight you have lost. When your metabolism is sufficiently high, you should begin dieting again, starting with 1 or 2 weeks on Phase I and then moving on to Phase II.

Your metabolism is sufficiently high when you can eat 2,000-3,000 calories a day and not gain weight. It may be necessary for you to cycle through the phases several times before reaching your goal weight.

Simply follow the Phase III method previously

described. In a month or two of mostly eating, you will have stabilized at this new weight. Your metabolism should be sufficiently high to allow you to begin losing weight again.

LOW METABOLISM

If you have been yo-yo dieting or have been dieting perpetually, you may have sabotaged your metabolism. You should disregard Phases I and II and begin with Phase III in order to raise metabolism. The process is the same. Your current weight will be your low or ideal weight and you should select a high weight that is a few pounds higher. Begin to eat at a caloric level that is high enough to raise your metabolism. Never gain more than a few pounds, then lose them by using the Phase I diet for two or three days. As your prevailing metabolism is raised, you should be able to eat normally for longer periods of time, before you reach your high weight and must diet again.

When your metabolism is sufficiently high to start losing weight you may follow the normal program, beginning with Phase I.

CONGRATULATIONS

I hope you have enjoyed great success with this program. There are many ways to measure your success other than just the scale. Your clothes fit better. People are noticing that you look different. You have more energy and you feel better about yourself. Even if you are not at your ultimate goal, you have come a long way. The best part is that you need never regain any of the weight that you lost. You protected your lean tissue and have raised metabolism back to pre-diet levels.

You have set yourself up for long-term success with your health, nutrition and weight-loss goals. Enjoy it!

God Bless,

Gary Heavin,
Founder & C.E.O.
Curves International, Inc.

INDEX

INDEX

INDEX

NOTES